ADVANCE PRAISE

"*Efficiency Bitch* is not only a practical guide to 'having it all,' but it's witty, smart, and will make any woman today feel seen, understood, and motivated to stop doing it all."

–Sarah Walton, leadership coach and founder of Bettermeant

"Melissa's framework for being an *Efficiency Bitch*, along with the innumerable practical suggestions for making my life more efficient, are both amazing and humbling. Why didn't I think of that?! Oh, because I never gave myself a minute to. Read this book and you'll give yourself all the minutes you need!"

–Jessie Lane Hunt, owner of Rio Strategies Consulting

"I LOVE *Efficiency Bitch!* I realized after reading the book that 'Efficiency Bitch' is a moniker I need to liberally adopt for myself. Melissa has done a fantastic job of breaking down a complex subject into bite-sized chunks in a very human and relatable way while providing actionable insights for lessons that anyone can easily adopt."

–Victoria Pelletier, corporate executive, keynote speaker, and author

"I wish this book had been available when I was starting out, or even mid-career. It's packed full of fantastic ideas, tips, and tricks that I and many other women had to learn the hard way."

–Kim Davis, retired HR executive and co-owner of Ivy & Sage Home and Lifestyle Co.

"If you're a woman struggling to find balance and freedom in this crazy thing we call life, this book is for YOU! *Efficiency Bitch* is the perfect blend of humor, wisdom, and practical application to important life skills. Easy to read and full of surprises, Melissa shares her secrets to truly being THE Efficiency Bitch."

–Nichole Hazuka, Physician Assistant; CEO of Nutritiously Fit4Life

"This book was filled with tangible steps alongside stories that really paint the picture of how to make small changes to find more of your inner EB. Couldn't put it down."

—Amanda Larson, CMO Smudge Pot Direct

"Whether we're a parent, caregiver, teacher, ally, or boss, we can only take others as far as we've gone ourselves. After reading *Efficiency Bitch*, I was clear that Melissa has put in the work. She writes with clarity and conviction. Her message is intentional, timely, and dare I say it, *efficient*. Her book offers a methodology that, if followed, will change lives. You cannot read *Efficiency Bitch* and not experience a shift in your perception about work, life, and sustainable success."

—Chris Tompkins, author of *Raising LGBTQ Allies: A Parent's Guide to Changing the Messages from the Playground*

"A must read for all women who want to be equipped with practical tips and tune in with themselves to raise their children to become the leaders of this new generation! Melissa Leon's stories are inspiring, her message is clear, and the tips are super simple to implement. Brilliant work Melissa!"

—Jocelyn Chong, MBA, GAICD; CEO and founder of Seed to Sequoia, #1 international best-selling author

"As a working mother of three girls, I wish I had this book years ago! Working mom's experience so much angst moving up the ranks and juggling life with children. Melissa's real-life stories are relatable and her worksheets to plan your first steps to change are the perfect tools to support success. My girls are grown and in the early phase of their careers. I plan on giving them a copy to support them as they soar to new heights in both their careers and family life."

—Karen Welch, retired former Vice President Total Rewards, Four Seasons Hotels and Resorts

"*Efficiency Bitch* is perfect for any ambitious woman. Melissa gives great advice in a simple, non-complicated way. Wish I'd had this book when I was starting out in my career."

–Ilse Harley, Regional Vice President and General Manager, Four Seasons Hotels

"The title of Melissa Leon's book, *Efficiency Bitch*, immediately challenged my inner perfectionist. I discovered EB was an invitation to challenge my perspective rather than add to my overflowing cup of 'to-do's.' The book is smart, funny, and Melissa is so relatable. The pages kept turning themselves."

–Lauryn Moeser, behavioral health professional

"Bright, breezy *Efficiency Bitch* is packed with pragmatic tips and strategies for young, ambitious women who want a robust life. Never preachy or patronizing, Melissa Leon's lively, honest style brings fresh perspectives to managing family, career, money, a household, and volunteering—all aimed at honing an ambitious woman's mindset and habits to get the most from life. Her sections on money and technology management are especially relevant."

–Ann Brown, retired newspaper editor

"Melissa has an incredible way of sharing her wisdom that is easy to understand and apply. As a female entrepreneur myself, she makes what could be complex areas of life simpler. This book will truly empower you to live out your dreams—having it all while not sacrificing it all! I have officially joined the EB Tribe."

–Kat Mills, wife, mom, businesswoman, and entrepreneur

"I was trying to do it all. Reading EB has been the first step in my journey to mental enlightenment. It's the book I didn't know I needed."

–Jennifer Chavez, cloud architect, wife, mother

"*Efficiency Bitch* is a phenomenal blueprint for women and mothers everywhere about how to tangibly embrace their dreams, be all they can be, and become the living, breathing example for their children, showing them how they, too, can rise to become all they're meant to be. Nurturing women fully standing in their power is the missing link to our society elevating to greater levels of humanity. Melissa is a force of nature, and I'm so happy to see her teaching others to do so as well!"

—Keli Raymond, owner of Pathway Hypnotherapy and Intuitive Counseling

"As a college student looking toward a big future, this book lays out a pathway for me to create an amazingly successful career and a fantastic family. Melissa shows it's not about trying to 'do it all' but about having a happy and balanced life where there's always room for that big career and a happy family. A must-read for every young professional."

—Riley Loughery, Grand Canyon University student

"Melissa doesn't shy away from talking about hard things that we're all thinking about as busy women. She also doesn't pretend that her way is the best or only method. Instead, *Efficiency Bitch* offers valuable insight into Melissa's thought process and systems. Readers can discern for themselves the best path forward."

—Leslie Woodard, Director of People

"A guidebook for the busy woman! So many tricks, tools, and ideas to keep your buckets from overflowing."

—Megan Humphreys, Vice President, Food & Beverage Strategy

"A no nonsense book about how to have it all without doing it all. I especially enjoyed the Bank section with easy to implement techniques to determine 'Money Available To Save or Spend' (MATS)."

—Marrianne Gill, Vice President, PNC Bank

EFFICIENCY BITCH™

HOW AMBITIOUS WOMEN CAN HAVE IT ALL WITHOUT DOING IT ALL

MELISSA LEON

EFFICIENCY BITCH™

HOW AMBITIOUS WOMEN CAN HAVE IT ALL WITHOUT DOING IT ALL

MELISSA LEON

Peacock Proud
PRESS

PHOENIX, ARIZONA

Efficiency Bitch™: How Ambitious Women Can Have It All Without Doing It All
Copyright © 2022 by Melissa Leon

First Published in the USA in 2022 by Peacock Proud Press, Phoenix, Arizona
  ISBN 978-1-957232-11-9 Hardback
  ISBN 978-1-957232-12-6 Paperback
  ISBN 978-1-957232-14-0 eBook
Library of Congress Control Number: 2022918992

Editors
  Laura L. Bush, PhD, peacockproud.com
  Alisa Sever
  Taryn Blanchard

Cover and Interior Layout
  Jana Linnell

Portrait Photographer
  Rachel Elizabeth Mostofizadeh, rachelelizphoto.com

DISCLAIMER: This is a work of nonfiction. The information is of a general nature to help readers know and understand more about becoming an Efficiency Bitch. Readers of this publication agree that Melissa Leon will not be held responsible or liable for damages that may be alleged or resulting directly or indirectly from their use of this publication. All external links are provided as a resource only and are not guaranteed to remain active for any length of time. The author cannot be held accountable for the information provided by, or actions resulting from accessing these resources.

TABLE OF CONTENTS

PREFACE: THE EFFICIENCY BITCH ORIGIN XIII

INTRODUCTION: THE FIVE PILLARS OF THE
EFFICIENCY BITCH MINDSET 1

B – Bank 4

I – Inbox 5

T – Time 5

C – Connection 5

H – Harmony 5

Random Happenstance 6

CHAPTER 1: A NEW KIND OF BITCH 9

Bitch 9

Feminist Waves 10

Future Waves 12

The Invisible Load 15

CHAPTER 2: B for BANK 22

Paycheck Friday 24

Money Available to Spend (MATS) 27

Allowance 30

Calculate your Money Available to Spend (MATS) 32

Wealth Management 34

On the Road to Financial Freedom 38

Credit Cards and Credit Scores 41

New Generations, New Ideas 45

CHAPTER 3: I for INBOX 49

Touch It Once 50

Never Rely on Memory 51

Embrace Imperfect Action 52

Use technology. 53

Declutter 57

Travel Smarter 59

CHAPTER 4: T for TIME **62**

Delegate 64

Automate 71

Eliminate 82

CHAPTER 5: C for CONNECTION **86**

You Are What You Eat. 86

It Takes a Village 87

Find Your Tribe 89

Support The Cause 92

The Art of Persuasion 95

CHAPTER 6: H for HARMONY **101**

Locus of Control 103

Try New Things 104

Mom Wars 105

Glass Balls. 110

CONCLUSION: FALL IN LOVE WITH YOUR FUTURE SELF . **114**

ACKNOWLEDGMENTS **116**

ABOUT THE AUTHOR **119**

NOTES **121**

To my husband, Steve, for loving me just the way I am,
seeing through my imperfections,
and co-creating the amazing life we have together.

To my children: my Butterfly, my Bird, my Sun.
You are my greatest creations,
and I cannot wait to see who you become.

THE EFFICIENCY BITCH ORIGIN

During my first visit home from college, my parents threw a tailgate party for the University of Arizona Homecoming football game. My parents *love* to host parties; we had them a lot growing up. My mom is the kind of woman who always sees the little things. Her attention to detail makes a party go from good to great. She thinks ahead, anticipates the needs of others, and puts their comfort on her to-do list. Ninety-nine percent of what she does goes completely unnoticed by her party guests, but the impact is significant. And it's not just her party planning skills. She has this level of consideration for others all the time, and she's terrific at it.

My mom is so detail-oriented that she carefully planned the University of Arizona Homecoming football game by the minute. She knew what to do and in what order, ensuring we each had an assigned job. At least, that's how I remember it.

So, we're thirty minutes to kickoff. My sister, fourteen at the time, was working hard, almost done cleaning the guest bath. My brother, sixteen, hurried to move our cars to the side of the house, his usual pre-party assignment. My dad was tidying up the yard and putting the dogs in their den.

And I was…there. As an eighteen-year-old college freshman, I hadn't planned to attend the party. I'd say hello to my parents' friends, then meet up with mine. Not in a hurry to do anything or go anywhere, I watched my mom enter the kitchen. She was a woman on a mission: fully dressed, with her makeup and hair done, which meant guests would be arriving shortly.

Mom had a predictable routine for entertaining, one I had seen many times before. First, clean up the house, make the beds, shower, and run to the grocery store while her hair air-dried. Next, arrive home, unload the groceries, and stage the items she needed for the party. Then, finish any last-minute cleanup, take out the trash, check the guest bathroom, and head to her room for hair, makeup, and clothes. Finally, organize all the food and drink for the guests.

My mother always said she did not want to be tending house or in the kitchen when her guests were over; she wanted to be with them, so she prepared everything in advance.

As I stood in the kitchen, eighteen and feeling wildly independent, I made myself my favorite snack: peanut butter spread thin on a tortilla, rollup style. As I placed the butter knife in the sink, I heard, "Put everything back exactly where you found it."

I rolled my eyes. "Ok, Mom, I will," I said in a tone that warranted mom eye daggers.

No more than three steps into the hallway, tortilla rollup in hand, I heard, "Melissa, get back in here!"

Ugh. What does she want now?

I walked in and saw the fury on Mom's face. She frantically moved and repositioned items in the fridge, on the counter, and back and forth. Did I move the chips and salsa? I couldn't remember. Had I touched the fruit salad and left it on the counter? I didn't think so. She just wanted to pick a fight.

"I didn't touch that."

She gave me a stare. You know the one, the mom one.

"I told you not to touch anything. I have everything I need, and I'll run out of time if I have to redo it all. Everything has a place. I have a system, an efficient system, and if you're going to disrespect it, you can leave."

"Yep, you are efficient, all right, but you don't have to be such an Efficiency Bitch all the time!"

Oh, snap! That got her attention.

Her eyes darted to me. She sent me a silent signal, informing me that I'd started trouble. She didn't have time to let me have it because guests would be arriving soon. I knew the fight would continue after the party. I would have to wait until later that night or, even worse, the next day for the entire lecture and punishment.

I wasn't always the best teenager. I got into my fair share of trouble and tried to prove my independence on more than one occasion. My mom had heard me swear before, and it definitely wasn't welcomed. We didn't grow up allowed to swear, but we weren't sheltered from it either. I'd had a decent education in using swear words. I knew time and place were critical.

The next day came, and we still had not discussed the word I'd called her.

The pressure mounted. I sensed we would have one of our giant blow-ups, a signature trait of my adolescence. Another day went by—more silence. This was bad; I knew it. I'd been out of line before, but I could tell this one really pissed her off.

Sunday rolled around, and I'd be driving back to school later that afternoon. I sat on the couch watching television when she said, "I need to run some errands. Do you want to come? I promise not to be an Efficiency Bitch again."

We laughed. Mine, the nervous kind.

My mom was a police officer in her twenties—one of the first female officers in Tucson, I might add—and a fraud investigator for most of her career, so her interrogation skills were top notch. I hesitated at the idea of driving around town for a few hours but agreed to go anyway. We dropped off dry cleaning, went to the post office, and returned items at the mall. We said nothing more about the "B-word." Like it never happened.

A few weeks later, she used it casually in a phone conversation. More nervous laughter. I suggested that "EB" would be more appropriate to say in public, so we used that more frequently. Truth is, I wanted a way to say it without saying "the B-word." As tough and grown-up as I tried to seem, I felt uncomfortable swearing around my mom. I still am.

As I matured and my own EB started to show, she dubbed me EB2. My younger sister soon followed and became EB3. It became a form of bonding for us and something we all admire, encourage, and love about each other. Still is.

The truth is…I've always been a little high strung. High strung isn't necessarily a bad thing, but I focused my time and energy in all the wrong places. I wanted to have it all, so I did it all, and then some. If you knew me in my early EB days, you probably saw someone who looked like she had it all together. On the inside, though, I was miserable. An endless hamster wheel fueled by coffee, beer, and Zoloft. A few years after my third child was born, I hit rock bottom. Since then, I've climbed my way back up, achieving more success, happiness, and good health than I could have ever imagined.

Over the last few years, I have walked the walk, tested, and defined the five pillars of becoming an Efficiency Bitch. You, too, have not only the ability to get it all done, but to master your money, time, and tasks and find the harmony you crave. In the coming chapters you will learn more about these five pillars and how to apply them in your life today, tomorrow, and for years to come. I'm thrilled that you're here—welcome to our "B-Hive."

INTRODUCTION
THE FIVE PILLARS OF THE EFFICIENCY BITCH MINDSET

I've always wanted a big career and a big family, but it wasn't always obvious to me how to have it all without doing it all. Once I figured it out, I found the secret recipe to efficiency and am here to share the secret with you.

What is an Efficiency Bitch™?

She's a strong woman who is unstoppable in the pursuit of her dreams. An Efficiency Bitch (EB) is a positive influence.

She refuses to let gender norms, pressure from political ideologies, and cultural stigmas define her goals and life path. She uses self-reflection, others' ideas, and her instincts to drive change.

She strives for maximum productivity with minimum wasted effort or expense. She chooses the people in her life carefully and never allows anyone to dim her light. She manages her life to spend time with her family, her passions, and herself. She lifts others up, demanding the same level of expectation and opportunity.

She counts her blessings and knows that her life is different from everyone else's. She understands where she came from and knows where she is going. She takes responsibility for her path, her choices, and her future.

So who am I? I'm an Arizona native, happily married since 2009 to my best friend, Steve, and a mom of three young children. I spent seventeen years in the hotel industry and traveled the globe to climb the corporate ladder. I co-built a small bookkeeping and fractional CFO business, Two Sense Consulting: Time and Money Expertise for Small Businesses, from the ground up. I'm also a sister, daughter, friend, podcaster, and public speaker.

I earned a bachelor's degree in Hotel and Restaurant Management and a master's degree in Business Administration (MBA). I'm also a certified Project Management Professional (PMP). For recreation, I golf with my husband and go on road trips with my family—or, as my daughter calls it, "glamping"—in our little travel trailer. I volunteer my time as a member of the Board of Directors of Planned Parenthood Arizona and a ranch camp and retreat center for youth. I guest lecture on small business accounting and career development at local universities and high schools as often as I get invited.

I also have the honor and privilege of being a mentor to young women who want to have incredible careers and raise a family. These women are the inspiration for this book. My heart swells knowing they see me as a role model, guide, and inspiration for what their life might be like as they navigate their careers and become their best selves.

This book is not a step-by-step guide to cleaning your closet or managing your money (although I do love these things). Instead, it's a path forward to shifting your paradigm and focus to improve the life of your future self. Don't get me wrong. I'm not suggesting you live solely for the future. On the contrary, I'm suggesting you focus on improving areas of your life today so you can live your future more completely.

I wrote this book for every woman who asks herself:

- *"I love my career, but I don't feel I get to spend enough time with my kids. Do I have what it takes to do both?"*
- *"I'm doing too much. I have to give up something, but I love all the things I'm doing. Where do I start?"*
- *"I want to have kids one day. Can I have family and a career I love?"*

No matter what phase of life you're in, there's always room to improve. The grass is not greener on the other side, but it is greener where you water it. Finding newer, faster, easier ways to do the things you don't enjoy will clarify these choices. Women don't have to choose between their interests and their family. Men don't have to bear the brunt of being the provider. Both parents can follow their dreams and raise healthy, well-balanced children.

This book is jam-packed with tips, tricks and, more importantly, an approach to developing a mentality that will help you get exactly what you want. To keep you organized, I created a download to help you track the items you want to remember. It has prompts to help you recall what you read and space for you to write down how you will apply them. Download your free copy before you get too far in at **EfficiencyBitch.com/BHive**. I also have a page on my website with links to all the books, products, and resources I mention in this book. Because the world is always changing, I'll add new products over time, so check back often. You can find this at **EfficiencyBitch.com/FavoriteThings**.

In the following chapters, we will dig into the five pillars of the Efficiency Bitch mindset and lifestyle that you need to focus on to put your future self in the best place she can possibly be. My book helps ambitious women stop wasting time, money, and all their awesome potential so that they can become an Efficiency Bitch—a strong, unstoppable woman who is always growing and pursuing her dreams.

To optimize the content of this book, consider the message, not the task. To be truly efficient, you must always look for the root cause of the issue, the starting point, and the lead domino to set the rest in motion. I hope that when you finish reading this book, you understand how you can shift focus as you pass through each phase of life.

Think of the material in this book the same way you would read a "how to raise a puppy" book. You wouldn't bring home an eight-week puppy, read a book cover to cover, and assume you can teach the puppy everything she needs to know in a day. Nor a month. Nor even a year. Instead, you teach the puppy one thing at a time, beginning with something that will make communicating with her tomorrow easier.

First, you teach the puppy the name you want her to respond to. She doesn't know her name when you bring her home. Next, you begin the long process of potty training. These take a while, so you work on this over the next six months and add other tasks alongside it.

Soon, you teach the puppy how to walk on a leash. If you haven't had the insanely frustrating and rewarding experience of raising a dog from a puppy, trust me, the leash part is harder than it sounds. Then, you move on to sit, drop it, leave it, and come. As she gets older, you teach her to stay. While working on these commands, you introduce the puppy to new social situations so she can practice her tricks with distractions. Maybe you enroll her in a puppy class.

The puppy builds her knowledge based on her own experiences over time. After months of effort, the puppy is a happier, healthier dog. She knows how to avoid danger, come when called, and do a few tricks that make everyone pet her.

It will be a while before the puppy becomes a full adult dog. Still, the progress the puppy makes is notable and noticeable very quickly. Every training session, the puppy gets better, faster, and stronger.

Please don't think I'm implying you are a puppy. You are the trainer, training yourself. Take the information in this book one step at a time. Implement the fast tricks, know which ones will take more time, and be sure to develop a plan for where you are going. For example, do you want your puppy to grow up like a hunting hound, a show dog, or a family playmate? Same concept goes for you. You get to choose the path and decide on a training plan accordingly. Give yourself time. Don't expect perfection—imperfect action is the name of the game.

As I organized and transcribed my thoughts, my family title of EB kept ringing in my ears. So, I decided to formulate my message around it. Fortunately for me, the word "bitch" offers the perfect letters for a guiding acronym. The five pillars are not in a specific order of importance (except as the acronym B.I.T.C.H.). Each pillar is important in its own right and may shift in priority for you based on your personal circumstances.

B - BANK

Money should never be on your heart, but it should be on your mind. Understanding money is key to becoming an Efficiency Bitch because money touches everything. Anything you use, consume, or see could be sold or traded for money. Money is a topic that many people are uncomfortable talking about, and a pain point in their pursuit of happiness. Knowing how to manage your money and improve it in the future will provide the vehicle you need to maintain your vision. You will learn how to understand money, use it, and build a relationship with it so that it helps rather than hurts you.

I – INBOX

Our lives are one big inbox. In fact, it's called that because there is always something in it. Everything we do has an inflow and an outflow, from our education and homes to our marriage and children. This includes the actual inboxes—mail, email, texts, and the physical tray sitting on your desk. It also consists of the inbox in your brain that you create for yourself and your ever-growing to-do list. You'll learn how to manage and simplify your inbox (and, therefore, the flow of your outbox), which will provide the mental and calendar clarity to chase your dreams.

T – TIME

Time is the great equalizer. Regardless of where we live in the world, we all have the same number of hours in a day. How you spend your time impacts what fills your day. You'll master how to think about the time you spend on tasks and how to optimize it. You'll take away concrete actions that will help you stay ahead of schedule rather than run behind. My secret recipe: delegate, automate, eliminate.

C – CONNECTION

One of the incredible opportunities that we have, as humans, is the ability to connect and support one another. Of course, we all do it a little differently. You will learn how the human connections you make impact your efficiency in negotiations, making friends, and using volunteer time to enrich your life. Carefully selecting the people you spend time with will enhance your overall efficiency.

H – HARMONY

Harmony is what we are after. This means different things to different people at different times in life. The key is defining what harmony means for you.

Initially, I titled this pillar "Health," followed by "Happiness." Neither fully fit. While health and happiness are certainly part of this pillar, the goal is harmony. It's all intertwined and interdependent. As you begin to understand how your health is impacted by your ability to manage your inbox, your happiness by your ability to manage your bank, and your connections to your time management, you'll discover how harmony is the icing on the cake that simply cannot be left out. Your mental, physical, and spiritual health play so heavily into overall efficiency that it deserves a category all its own.

As we dive into each of these pillars, remember that they are not in order of importance. They all intersect and impact you. My life changed the day I fell in love with my future self, and I've committed to always putting her well-being first, no matter what. To help demonstrate the strength of the B-Hive, I've connected with some women who have learned valuable lessons along the way. You'll see the messages they have for you sprinkled throughout the book. I hope you find them as inspiring as I do.

> *"Always remember you are stronger than you think you are, and you can do anything you set your mind to. Seeking fulfillment in life takes risk and action, and everyone's purpose is different."*
> **Wanda Tompkins, mother of two**
> **Operations Manager, Theara, Neurodiversity Wellness Educators**

RANDOM HAPPENSTANCE

While researching content for this book, my mom gave me a scrapbook created by my great-grandfather in 1975. It's a collection of letters, pictures, and stories he felt compelled to write around the time of his eighty-fifth birthday. I never met my great-grandfather, but reading his words made me feel connected to him. I noticed his attachment to nostalgia, history, and writing—all things I connect with. I am interested in my heritage, the people who came before me, and the stories of their lives.

To my surprise, the scrapbook contained a detailed family tree dating back to the first generation of immigrants in my family who came to the Americas. Hailing from England and Germany, my ancestors have been on this land since 1740. I found names and notes of family members who fought under George Washington in the War of 1812 and Civil War. While this type of historical information has always fascinated me, it gained new meaning this time. As they say, the teacher will appear when the student is ready.

The week before I saw the scrapbook, my publisher suggested I read *White Fragility: Why It's So Hard for White People to Talk About Racism*,[1] by Robin DiAngelo. The book offered new perspectives on race and the privileges of being white that I had never considered. DiAngelo describes the system that keeps racism intact and the system that keeps white people from noticing. It opened my eyes to how affirmative action has benefitted white women more than any other minority group. She writes, "although we are taught that women were granted suffrage in 1920, we ignore the fact that it was white women who received full access or that it was white men who granted it. Not until the 1960s, through the Voting Rights Act, were all women—regardless of race—granted full access to suffrage. Naming who has access and who doesn't guides our efforts in challenging injustice."[2]

As I read *White Fragility* and explored my great grandfather's scrapbook, I realized that a large portion of my success is due to the random happenstance of being born a white American. I wanted to write a book about how to do it all, be it all, and still have the energy to chase three children—when I realized that not everyone has access to my reality.

I chose to write the book I set out to write, and I offer it to you with the utmost respect and appreciation for the life you live and were born into. I cannot change the environment I came from any more than you can, but I acknowledge that each of our lives is different. We were born, without choice, in the city where our mothers lived and inherited parts of the culture that surrounded us. Whatever your circumstance, I hope you see this book as encouragement to keep fighting for what is possible for you, your children, and your grandchildren.

The only thing we all have in common is that we came into this world via a woman. What happens before and after that point of entry is different for each of us.

To become an Efficiency Bitch, you'll need to have a clear direction, something to work toward. Each of the five pillars you'll explore will build upon each other to shape your best future self.

Before we dive into the five pillars, let's look at how we (ambitious women) got here. By learning a tiny part of feminist history, we can begin to understand why our grandmothers and mothers taught us the things they did. Becoming aware of the past will help us uncover some of the current gender norms and social stigmas that working women face every day.

In the next chapter, we'll explore the connection between efficiency, the history of the word "bitch," feminism, gender norms, and women's rights. If you are eager to dive into the five pillars of B.I.T.C.H., I invite you to jump to Chapter 2, B for Bank.

> *"Those who criticize you are not walking out your life challenges, in your shoes, ever. Give up on maintaining perfection in all areas of your life and accept the blessings of where you are and what you have accomplished."*
>
> **Amy Rose Herrick, mother of six**
> **Chief Executive Officer, The Secret Profits**

CHAPTER 1

A NEW KIND OF BITCH

BITCH

As a professional and a mother, I had to think twice about writing a book with the word "bitch" on the cover. I kept thinking, *do I want to write a book that spotlights a word used to insult women?* When I tested the title on social media and to my friends, I received a variety of responses. Some people loved it. Some laughed it off. Others were all out against it. I needed to do more research to make a final decision.

> *Merriam-Webster* defines "bitch" as:
> **noun**
> 1. the female of the dog or some other carnivorous mammals
>   *informal + often offensive:* a malicious, spiteful, or overbearing woman
>   *informal + offensive:* used as a generalized term of abuse and
>   disparagement for a woman
>   *informal:* something that is extremely difficult, objectionable,
>   or unpleasant
>
> **verb**
> 2. spoil, botch (bitched)
>   cheat, double-cross (bitching)
>   to complain of or about (bitches)[3]

"Bitch" can also be an adjective, although I didn't find that in the dictionary. This connotation was more common in the 1960s and again in the 1980s: "That concert was bitchin' (*awesome*)!" "That was the bitchiest (*negative*) thing I've ever seen." And then, of course, all the funny idioms:

- Resting Bitch Face: a woman who looks upset while at rest
- Life's a bitch: life is hard

- Bitch slap: to slap someone open-handed across the face
- Flip a bitch: a U-turn while driving
- Son of a bitch: an exclamation used when you stub your toe or an insult to a man, indicating his mother is a bitch

The history of the word is so comical that a television comedy series called *History of Swear Words* dedicates an entire episode to it.[4] Consider doing your own research on the history of the word "bitch." You'll find a range of assumptions about how it developed over time, but most seem to follow this timeline: The current pronunciation of the word as we know it developed from the Old English word *bicce* or *bicge*, which means "female dog" and dates to around 1000 CE. The word is rarely used in this context in modern times unless you breed dogs. How the term came to apply to human women is speculative. Some research indicates it began in 1400 CE when referring to promiscuous women. According to language historian Geoffrey Hughes, this was when being called a "son of a bitch" first became associated with the implication that the addressee's mother was a prostitute.[5]

FIRST WAVE

Using "bitch" as an insult didn't become truly popular until the first wave of feminism began in the United States in the late 1800s and early 1900s.[6] That's when men (and probably some women) used it to insult annoying women who were fighting for their right to vote. They were perceived as aggressive, irritating, and obstructive. They dared to challenge the status quo and needed to be mocked for it. Between 1915 and 1930, the use of the word in newspapers more than doubled.[7] It soon became an all-purpose insult for annoying, belligerent, unreasonable, malicious, controlling, aggressive, or dominant women.

SECOND WAVE

Between the 1960s and 1980s, the second wave of the feminist movement broadened to take on a range of women's legal and societal rights. Influential books like *The Bitch Manifesto* (1968), by Jo Freeman, reappropriated the word "bitch."[8] Freeman wrote, "We must be strong, we must be militant, we must be dangerous. We must realize that Bitch is Beautiful and that we have nothing to lose." She adds, "A Bitch occupies a lot of psychological space. You always know she is around. A Bitch takes shit from no one. You may not like her, but you cannot ignore her." This changed the drive and behavior of some women. It encouraged them to challenge the norm and consider that they could have an identity outside their family. As a result, the use of the word began to change as women took on new roles.

THIRD WAVE

The third feminist wave began in the 1990s when Anita Hill testified that Clarence Thomas, who would go on to be confirmed as a Supreme Court Justice, had sexually harassed her. Women continued the fight for their rights, including equality in the workplace and the redefinition of sexual harassment. Enacted during this wave, the Family and Medical Leave Act (FMLA) of 1993 protects employees who require time off due to medical reasons for themselves or their families.[9] The law provides protection (not pay) if you take maternity leave, have surgery, or need to care for a loved one.

Prior to FMLA, it was commonplace for women to leave the workforce during the early years of a child's life and return when they were school age. Today, the FMLA provides an employee up to fourteen weeks of unpaid job security. Length of employment and medical proof are required to receive this security, but this is a massive benefit that employees did not previously have. There's an ongoing debate about whether this protected leave should be paid, and, if so, by whom. Some believe it should be a social benefit paid for by the state or federal government, but others believe it should be paid for by an employer. As of 2022, the United States ranks last among wealthy countries in their maternity leave policy.[10]

FOURTH WAVE

While the #MeToo hashtag was coined by sexual assault survivor and activist Tarana Burke in 2006, it took more than a decade for the movement to gain traction, go global, and become a lasting part of our society.[11] January 21, 2017, approximately four and a half million people attended

Women's Marches across the United States, the largest single-day demonstration in the country's history, which helped propel #MeToo to mainstream media.[12] Finally in October 2017, celebrities such as Alyssa Milano, Uma Thurman, and Gwyneth Paltrow used their voices—along with the hashtag #MeToo—to call attention to survivors of sexual harassment and sexual violence. This movement brought to light many long-standing acts of misconduct by powerful, wealthy men such as Bill Cosby, Harvey Weinstein, Kevin Spacey, and Larry Nassar.

FUTURE WAVES

Feminism and the fight for gender equality is a complex sociopolitical topic, and our fight for equality is far from over. Our children and grand-children will have to continue the fight. The point of my message in this chapter is not to oversimplify this very complex matter, but rather to reflect on how we as a culture of women have evolved over the last century. I am extremely passionate about the protection of women's rights and our future —and only more so in 2022 after the Supreme Court of the United States overturned Roe v. Wade and the federal protection to safe and legal abortion. Regardless of your position on abortion, I'd invite you to take it as one example of how every "right" that the women who came before us fought for can be taken away. We must never become complacent.

The word "bitch" has evolved alongside the feminist movements, in certain contexts becoming synonymous with the word "feminist." The word feminist has in turn taken on the meaning of "man-hater" to some. I'm here to end the idea that feminists and self-proclaimed bitches are man-haters. Instead, I preach the opposite. Feminists see the value that all people bring to the world. I'm raising a little man and two little women. I pledge to teach all of them to see the value in the others, embrace their differences, and rejoice in their individual and collective similarities.

Through Two Sense Consulting, and as part of my passion for financial literacy, I often speak about basic accounting and money management to small business owners. In my speaker bio, I include my titles of podcaster, author, and feminist. After one event, the participants took a survey and provided feedback. One person wrote, "Melissa made an unprofessional comment that she is a feminist. As a man, I feel this word is inappropriate in this setting." During our post-program review, the event management team read this feedback. Some people laughed at the comment. But I saw his point. Because "feminist" has transformed into "bitch," many now hear it as "man-hater." The participant thought I said, "I hate men." If I were him, I'd be offended, too. But that is not my message; it's the opposite. I am a feminist, yes. I will fight for equality, but it is not specific to women. My goal is to redefine "feminist" so that when the word is heard, it means a person fighting for equality across the board.

In the past, I've been afraid to be labeled a feminist. I didn't want to be perceived as a bra-burning man-hater. As a mother, I see the imbalance that the past feminist movements have curated for young men. My younger daughter loves music, and I made her a playlist of all her favorite songs for her birthday. She calls them her "girl-power songs." One day we were riding in the car listening to it, and my son said, "Mom, how come there are no boy-power songs?" I didn't have the right words to answer him at the time, but the truth is, an artist would likely be scrutinized for writing a "boy-power song." So, while I know why "girl-power" is needed (to advance equality), it doesn't mean young boys who don't have cheerleading anthems aren't impacted.

Well-meaning corporate "Women in Leadership" initiatives have also created awkward reward systems for promoting women to executive roles. While the intentions are good, they often leave women feeling like a focus group; a checkbox to fill a quota. Adding incentive encourages positive change, but it can also produce a stigma. In the 1970s, if a woman were in charge, some people wondered, "Who did she sleep with to get that job?" Today, people might say, "She got that job to fill a quota." Countless examples of why diversity is needed in every organization exist, but incentivizing these initiatives can create another social issue.

It's been said that American women have more freedom compared to women in other countries. While this may be true, and I am thankful, I also refuse to accept the status quo. We must keep pushing every day for complete equality, not just for American women but for women around the world. Without mindfully educating our sons and daughters, the work of past feminists is wasted. I challenge us to rise together, and make small changes today that will impact our children forever. Being a feminist means standing up for our daughters *and* our sons. We must stand together to understand where we come from, what life has taught us, and offer equal opportunity to all who are willing to work for it.

As I write this book, I feel confident in the label "bitch." I do understand and appreciate other women's discomfort when they hear this word. My perspective and the way I share the word with you is to describe a strong woman or person who stands up for their beliefs. Suppose the speaker chooses to use "bitch" in a derogatory sense, but the listener chooses to take it with a powerful meaning. In that case, the listener controls how it impacts them. I am armed with the entire history of its many uses, and I am proud to say I will continue the tradition of strong women.

When I started developing the Efficiency Bitch podcast, one of my first steps was to create social media profiles. As a result of the polarizing 2020 political landscape, the leading social media platforms updated their policies for words considered hate speech. When I initially used the word "bitch," every one of my posts got rejected by the Facebook and Instagram algorithms. I realized that while I've made peace with the word, others may not have; some sensitivity may be needed. There's a time and place for the use of "bitch," and a time when it can be abbreviated. Therefore, in public, on most of my swag, podcast, and social media, I use Efficiency B and EB to abbreviate Efficiency Bitch. I've also taken on a "Bee" persona and theme to my messaging. My intro to the podcast has often included, "You've heard of a honeybee, a busy bee, and a queen bee…This is Efficiency B." If you are one of the women who is not ready to use the word "bitch" when describing yourself, I understand. I hope you will find one of the alternatives and join our B-Hive just the way you are.

Understanding the past waves of feminism and how they have shaped the society we grew up in is important to becoming an EB. Without understanding why we feel obligated to "do it all," we won't be able to let go of the things we should in order to "have it all." The women of the past lived a different reality than we do today, and our children will live different realities in the future. We must prepare to explore the difference between what society and culture assigned to us and what we want to do as professionals, mothers, and women.

> *"Motherhood is different for every single one of us, and it can change with time. I went into motherhood expecting to have all the joy and fulfillment I perceived others as having. And I found that it didn't work for me (and likely them either). I've come to embrace that I love my child and am the best mother that I can be, but that doesn't mean I want to be mom-me all the time. Sending my kiddo to preschool and having sitters/nannies has been great for both of us. Our time together is that much more enjoyable, and our time apart is a positive thing."*

Lucy Petlack, mother of one
Lifestyle Influencer @lucismorsels

THE INVISIBLE LOAD

In addition to my seventeen years in the hotel industry, I spent four years studying it in college. As part of my school labs and manager-in-training rotation, I worked in the housekeeping department. Do you know who primarily operates the housekeeping departments of hotels? Women. There are men, but not many. Typically, men are the "housemen." They run clean towels and linens to rooms and strip the beds of the dirty ones. Is that sexist? I don't think so; it's who applies for the jobs. But why do women apply for housekeeping jobs while men don't? The more I pull at that thread, the longer it gets. The short answer is, women have been trained over centuries to be the gender that tends the nest while their male counterparts protect it.

While the history of feminism may not seem important to efficiency at first glance, we must know where we've been, to have a clear picture of where we're going. Women in the U.S. have been in a constant cycle of change since 1910. With each cycle, women have taken on more opportunities, challenges, and responsibilities. I am one of the oldest millennials (a generation that begins in the early 1980s). From my lens, I see the women before me who felt they had to choose between a career and a family. If they were brave enough to attempt both, they became subject to the popular buzzword "burnout." I refuse to choose, and I reject the possibility of burnout. I won't let the badass women of the past down by giving up or repeating the cycle of the impossible.

As a child, I absorbed the rules of the patriarchy from society, but had parents who wanted different things for me. My mom says the only thing she ever wanted for me was independence and confidence. My dad insisted I have trucks to play with, and both refused the pink trends for raising a daughter. Their desire for my independence came true; I have that in spades. My confidence took some time to develop, but eventually I had that too. Still, the invisible load that I picked up from society crept its way into my mind.

If you have children, you don't need me to tell you about the invisible load; you feel it. It's all the things you inventory, coordinate, and project manage for your family every day. And I'm not talking about the big, obvious stuff like homework and doctor appointments. I'm talking about the little things like knowing where everything is so the moment someone needs it you can pull it out of a hat. Or rotating the clothes for the kids every month to manage their growth spurts. Making sure everyone brushes their teeth, bathes, washing sheets and towels, decorating for holidays, monitoring screen time, sensory development, social development, and bedtime. It's all the things we just do because it must be done. I know when I'm carrying too much of the invisible load because I will have incredible clarity at the weirdest times, like in the shower, driving, or in the middle of the night. Things I need to do (or that I forgot to do) seem to jump up and bite me. I realized that this is when things sneak up on me because I'm not carrying as much of the load during these moments and my brain can finally process the little things.

A lot goes into being a mother and I don't resent it, but I do resent the disproportionate volume of these types of tasks that have fallen on us over decades as women entered the workforce. I don't agree with the argument that "women are just better at it." Rather, historically, I believe that we felt it was expected of us, so we got better all that work and passed it on to the next generation of women. Efficiency, coupled with a little intention and guidance, might just be a secret weapon to get us off the hamster wheel. We are the product of generations of women who had no choice but to get better and faster at *everything* just to find space to think. In pursuit of becoming an Efficiency Bitch, we will uncover not only the ability to get it all done, but also the ability to ask for help, delegate, and focus on the important things.

> **"** *The key to a fulfilling career starts with balance…*
> *and the ability to delegate.* **"**
>
> **Kelly Smutny, mother of three**
> **Director of Catering and Conference Services**

When Kamala Harris, the first woman Vice President of the United States, was sworn in, an overwhelming feeling of emotion came over me. I'm not sure what the emotion is called. It wasn't pride, excitement, or admiration. It was some combination of them all. For the first time, I saw my silhouette, a woman's profile, second in command. That had never happened before. It's not about her politics; it's the simple fact that this was a new achievement for a woman.

Several of my family's black friends flew to Washington, D.C., to attend Barack Obama's inauguration. I remember wondering why they would fly across the country for it. It's not like they *knew* him. But now I understand. For the first time, they saw someone who looked like them in a position that they had never held before. So many have said, "You can't be what you can't see." After this experience, I better understand the truth of that idea now. When I saw Kamala Harris sworn in, I felt it. I felt it for me…and I really felt it for my daughters.

My daughters will grow up, change, and explore their highly formative years (ages ten to eighteen) with a different perspective than any other

American generation before them. For the first time, a woman presides over the Senate and is next in line to become President of the United States. And while the external messages we receive from friends, media, government, and school impact our perception of the world, so do the messages we receive at home.

They also see a father cook dinner and their mother travel for work. Their parents are co-breadwinners and co-parents. Both parents take time for themselves and to be together. Both share household responsibilities, decision-making, and maintaining balance within themselves and their marriage.

In my formative years, I learned the value of my body when Anita Hill accused Justice Clarence Thomas of sexual harassment during his nomination to the Supreme Court. My generation learned "no means no" and demanded protection and consequences for violating our bodies. We were witness to laws that protect family medical care and prosecute violence against women. We grew up to be the women of the #MeToo movement. We demanded parental leave for adoptive parents, fathers, and mothers. We insisted that forced sex with a spouse equals rape and should be illegal. We demanded sexual harassment policies be established and our right to serve in the U.S. military. We became career-motivated and finally made up more than fifty percent of all college graduates in the U.S.

My mother, however, learned a different lesson at age ten. She entered her formative years in the 1960s when things were anything but equal in terms of both race and gender. Women had few career choices; they were nurses, teachers, waitresses, or housewives. They were responsible for the home and children, while men were responsible for bringing home a paycheck. In 1964, the Civil Rights Act was signed, making it illegal for employers to discriminate based on race or sex. Women of her era learned girls can be anything they want to be. They led the way on reproductive rights and birth control and reclaimed the term "bitch" as a power word for women of action. They demanded that young girls play sports, be allowed to apply for a credit card, and dream of having a career. Although initially encouraged to be a schoolteacher, my mother became one of ten female police officers to graduate from the police academy in Tucson, Arizona, in 1977.

My mom's choice to become a police officer shocked my grandmother. My grandmother didn't understand the need to go to college and work; she saw it as a man's role. My grandmother knew women deserved more rights, but the feminist movement of the 1960s and 1970s seemed outrageous. My grandmother was ten years old in 1925. Her generation saw triumphs like women winning the right to vote and, if married, the right to own land. However, these women learned hard lessons in poverty and autonomy as their husbands and fathers lost their jobs during the Great Depression and left for World War II and the Korean War. These women were often not educated past grade four and were taught only to take care of their home and children.

History is complicated. It's never told in full color because there are so many angles and truths to consider. Was it fair, in today's sense of the word, that women could not vote? Hell no! But were the men of the 1800s bad people for preventing women from voting? I don't think so. Rather, norms and expectations were completely different. Many women didn't even know they were missing something—until one day they did. Then they fought to get there and woke others up too. I see the same in the social movements today. You cannot see or understand how you are impacting another person until the lights get turned on. And once they are, and once you see the injustice that your comfort has put on another, well, you can't un-ring that bell.

We can't always understand the obstacles that someone else is experiencing if we have not experienced them. If you don't see the fence, how can you know it needs to come down? The key to moving forward is to make it safe to speak and listen about obstacles we face and help each other tear down those walls.

Not too long ago, my family attended an afternoon BBQ with four other families. Picture it: kids playing in the yard, four dads standing around the grill, and moms sitting in the living room, two of us with an infant on our boob. One of the women, Lauren, started telling a story of how her ten-year-old daughter felt upset that only the girls had to do the dishes after dinner while father and son didn't have to. Lauren shared that she had to explain to her daughter that this is just how the world works.

"Not that I agree with it," she said. "It sucks. But it's the way it is."

One of the other women tried to convince her otherwise. Still, she insisted that she would rather her daughter learn this lesson now than be disappointed later.

Lauren's primary argument was that no matter the changes we have seen in the last hundred years, women will always be subordinate to men. While I understand and can appreciate that she wants to prepare her daughter for the harsh reality of the patriarchy, I also see that she may be inadvertently perpetuating its existence. I agree that past generations have been raised this way and that there are many places in the world where women are still expected to hold certain roles. But the situation only perpetuates if we let it. Lauren could use this opportunity to show her children, both her son and her daughter, how it has been in the past, and that the cycle can be broken with them. As an Efficiency Bitch, I believe all family members hold the responsibilities of earning money, raising children, and taking care of a home.

While women's lives have shifted over the last one hundred years, so have men's lives. My grandfather's life, his reality, and his cultural norms were much different than my husband's today. And my son's life will also be different. I wish that our children, both girls and boys of all colors, shapes, sizes, and orientations, will live with open minds and the ability to see the obstacles others face and help make their world a better place.

Understanding how history impacted the women in your lineage and added to the invisible load you carry is critical. In the coming chapters, I'm going to talk a great deal about delegating and automating your workload. Start getting comfortable with the discomfort that comes with letting go of work that does not belong to you. Change is hard, and this kind will be no different. I invite you to think of this change as a bridge we're building that will shorten your commute to work. The construction will be annoying, you may get a flat tire from a stray nail, but every day more and more of the bridge will be complete. One day, seemingly out of nowhere, the on-ramp will open, and the new bridge of your dreams will be up and running full speed.

As we move into the B.I.T.C.H chapters, the real fun begins. The lead-off chapter is my personal favorite, but it's also the pillar that can make many people squirm: B for Bank.

"It might feel good in the moment to be the only one who can fix a peanut butter sandwich the right way or the only one who can coax a toddler into her pants, but if you don't give up control of little stuff, you will carry it all."

Ashley Quinto Powell, mother of two
Founder and CEO, myVA Rocks

CHAPTER 2
B for BANK

This topic, for me, is the most important. B is for Bank, but it's what's in the bank, that I'm interested in. Money makes the world go 'round. While you don't need to be rich to be happy, you need to know how money works. Knowing when to spend it, how to save it, and how to leverage it will make you live a more efficient life. When writing this book, I surveyed 100 parents aged 25-45. I asked them if they were confident in managing their money: 79 percent said, "No." Of that same group, I asked if they talk to their kids about money: 81 percent said, "No, not yet." I asked them if they were taught about money management at school, home, or neither: a whopping 94 percent said, "Neither." I don't blame schools. They have more to teach than there are hours in the day. I don't blame parents. How can you teach what you don't know? I don't blame anyone. It's no one's fault; but you can break the cycle. Don't skip this chapter no matter how uncomfortable it might make you feel.

Money touches everything. Look around you: everything in your home, the book you are reading, the clothes you are wearing, whatever you are sitting on, in, or under costs money. You or someone you know earned that money and decided to spend it on that item. Even if the item was a gift, someone somewhere spent money on it. The crazy thing is that, because money is such a taboo topic for many people, even the idea of this chapter might make you uncomfortable. While I do not believe we should have money on our hearts, we should have it on our minds.

Being wealthy is not about having a lot of money, but rather about being able to experience life the way you want to. Having the freedom to experience life comes from understanding money, not having a whole bunch of it. Unfortunately, I know far too many people who are in a perpetual cycle of panic because they don't know if they can pay their bills each month. Some tell me they don't get paid enough; some blame it on past debt. What they all have in common is that they don't have a solid understanding of how to use money to set themselves up for success. If you are one of these people, don't worry. You can get yourself back on track. If you are just starting out, make this your top priority. Your future self will thank you.

When someone asks what I do for a living, and I tell them that I'm an accounting and finance professional, they often respond with, "Oh, well, I'm really bad at math." It seems to be a reflex, in case I wanted to crunch numbers with them on the fly. But even those who do like math may not be great with money.

I used to be terrible at math. I failed Introduction to Accounting in my first year of college. Well, the truth is I didn't go to class because it started at seven in the morning on Fridays. Still, I told myself it had to be the math. And it wasn't the first time.

Somehow, I squeaked by in grades one to three, but in grade four my teacher realized I had fallen behind in math. My school separated math class by ability, so those who needed more help got it, and those who excelled could move at their own pace. I remember feeling embarrassed to be in the "bad at math group." One day, the teacher gave me two tests, the first in long division and the second in two-digit multiplication. I knew I would get the answers wrong and see the look of disappointment on her face. And, of course, I failed them both.

Immediately after, my teacher gave me two worksheets to practice before I retook the tests. Back at my desk, I got to work. Ten minutes later, I gave her the completed worksheets.

I remember the spiral-bound teacher's book with the answer keys. She went problem by problem with a stern look on her face and eventually wrote 100 percent on the first worksheet. Then, she moved to the next sheet. Same thing—100 percent! I was so excited, until I realized she still had a stern look on her face.

Finally, after what felt like forever, she pointed to the top-right corner of the sheet and showed me that the word "test" had been crossed off. She had tricked me. I had gotten 100 percent on two tests that were very similar to the ones I had failed moments before. My nine-year-old self didn't know what test anxiety meant, but soon learned that's what I had. My teacher and parents were thrilled. I didn't know what it all meant; if they were happy, though, it had to mean good things. I don't remember taking the tests or what thoughts I had while taking them, but from that point on, I never failed another math test (Freshman Accounting excluded).

Consider this your wake-up call. If you were once bad at money, you no longer are. BAM! Just like that. All you need is a little confidence. Read this chapter with an open mind about new ways you can build a relationship with your money. Learn about new tools and get the phrase "I'm bad with money" out of your head.

PAYCHECK FRIDAY

As a teenager, I could not wait to get a job. I craved freedom and responsibility and, yes, money. The day I turned sixteen, I began interviewing for jobs. I collected applications all over town and had calls back from two that I really wanted: Eegee's (a local Tucson sandwich shop) and Footlocker. My mom had another idea. She wanted me to apply at the bank where she worked as a fraud investigator. I had no interest. Being around all those adults and all that money freaked me out. But I wanted to please my mom, so like any good daughter, I applied for the job.

What happened next changed the trajectory of my life. I was offered a job as a flex-shift bank teller, way out of my league. I have no idea why the bank hired me. Maybe for the same reason I applied: as a favor to my mom. Either way, I felt intimidated. I felt weird being there. I worked Tuesday, Thursday, and Friday from 3:30 to 6:30 p.m. to support the "after-work rush hour." Online banking didn't exist in the mid-1990s, so bank branches were usually full of people.

About a week later, I received a job offer from Footlocker. I really wanted that one, for obvious teenager reasons. I couldn't decide between them, so I took both. I absolutely did not need two jobs; I had just turned sixteen. I did it anyway. I worked Footlocker on the weekends and the bank after school. I tolerated the bank. I didn't find this job as fun as Footlocker. The bank made me take so many training classes and read endless policies, pro-cedures, and memos. I also had to be fingerprinted and wear pantyhose (not cute tights, ugly uncomfortable control top pantyhose). At Footlocker, on the other hand, I fit right in. I got to wear the cute black-and-white striped uniform, hang stock as it came in, run the cash register, and flirt with boys.

Having these two jobs provided an incredible contrast for me. At Footlocker, I made minimum wage, $5.15 per hour at the time. At the bank, I made $9.00 an hour—almost twice the minimum wage. I worked more hours at Footlocker, but I made more money at the bank. I wanted to be at Footlocker, though, so I worked more hours there. Money was not my main motivator.

The job at the bank came with bigger responsibilities, such as handling other people's money, counting the money in the vault, and balancing my drawer. They paid more because the job had risk and responsibility and required more focus. For a while, Footlocker seemed like the more exciting of the two jobs, but as my friends got jobs and realized I worked at a bank, my social capital increased. Since a job at the bank seemed rare for a teen-ager, it also had more social value. Still not motivated by money, but very motivated by the "cool power" of the bank, I asked to have my hours in-creased and resigned from Footlocker.

Soon I learned the social patterns of things like Paycheck Friday. A typ-ical shift at the bank tallied about $5,000 in cash in/out, but Fridays always had $15,000 cash out and $0 cash in. People would stand in line for an hour, cash their whole paycheck, and deposit zero. Most of their bank balances had under $100. I didn't understand what they were doing with their money and why they wanted it all in cash. I never saw my parents with cash; they always used their checkbooks or debit cards. Then, I became friends with a co-worker who was five years older than me.

Twenty-one-year-old Jen was the single mother of a three-year-old son. Every other Friday, she would cash her entire paycheck and head to the supermarket to buy mountains of food. Once, I went with Jen and watched her fill the cart with mounds of *stuff*. It was like she was stocking up for the winter. Then, she would run to Old Navy to buy a new outfit to wear out with her friends that night—her one night a week without her baby. Every other Friday (payday), Jen was filled with confidence and excitement, but it wouldn't last.

By Tuesday of the following week, all the food had been eaten. Jen would resort to looking between couch cushions and under her car seat for gas money. Her confidence tanked; she'd seem miserable. She complained that she didn't have enough money to pay rent or bills or feed her son. She was stuck in a cycle of borrowing money from friends and family so she could get by, get paid, repay her loans, overspend, and then repeat the entire cycle.

Jen felt miserable when she had no money and seemed explosive when she had it. A single, young mother trying to learn along the way, but unable to get out of the cycle. She didn't know another way, or a way out. I wish I knew at the time and could have helped her see the crippling impact of being broke for twelve days and rich for two. I eventually lost touch with Jen, so I don't know what became of her and her son. If I had to guess, history repeated itself, and they lived that lifestyle for many years.

Modeling is the primary way we learn many things, including money management. Depending on the household you grew up in, you may have great spending habits or terrible ones. Either way, today is the day it no longer matters. Today is the day you take control of your financial dignity, create a plan to understand your money, and have as much as you need to live a life you love. Take the examples that your parents showed you (both the good and the bad) and build on them. Ask your parents to describe the ways they made ends meet when you were at home. If you don't have parents to talk to, ask a friend's parents. Hindsight is always 20/20, so asking someone older than you to share their money lessons will undoubtedly shed some light. Just keep in mind that money moves a little differently than it used to. People don't line up in banks to cash their checks, but the speed at which it exits their accounts is even faster. Autopay, debit cards, Venmo, and Zelle are conveniences that make it very easy to spend your "paycheck Friday money" on Thursday.

Reflect on your relationship with money and the ways you behave when you have a sudden windfall, or your funds are running low. To become an EB, you must understand your own relationship and behaviors when it comes to money. Once you know this, you can move on to the next step: learning how to spend and how to save.

MONEY AVAILABLE TO SPEND (MATS)

Have you ever noticed that time and money seem to expand and shrink to fit the container you keep them in? Your mind is not playing tricks on you. It's really happening. You can fold the laundry and put it away in ten minutes if you are in a rush. But if your favorite television show is on while you are folding, that same size load can take three times as long. Money is the same way. No matter how much money you make, you will always see your bank account expand and shrink. Therefore, you must never, expect money to save itself. Without intentional thought and direction, you will spend all your money without knowing it.

Steve and I lived in Hawaii in our early twenties. We had no kids, no mortgage, and no real responsibility. We both had full-time jobs that paid decent entry-level salaries. I worked in middle management in the accounting department at a luxury resort, and Steve worked at a local golf course. We lived in an 800-square-foot apartment, for which we paid $1,200 monthly. Steve's truck had been paid off, but I had a car payment of $300 a month. Our health insurance came from our paychecks, and our car insurance cost about $150 a month combined. We both held small credit card balances from our college days, and I had some student loan debt. Other than those expenses, the rest of our money could be spent at will.

Our monthly expenses looked something like this:

PER MONTH	
Net Paychecks	$ 3,000
Car Insurance	$ 150
Rent	$ 1,200
Car	$ 300
Utilities / Gas / Food	$ 500
Credit Card / Student Loans	$ 250
Money Available to Save (MATS)	$ 600

$2,400

$3,000 - $2,400 = $600

See the last line labeled Money Available to Save, "MATS." That's the focus of this chapter. MATS is the amount of money not allocated or assigned to an expense. It is not a representation of what you save, but money that could be saved if it's not spent. Think of it like French fries at the bottom of a fast-food to-go bag. The fries you *will* eat first are within easy reach. The fries you *might* eat are at the bottom of the bag. If you feel full, you may toss them in the trash. If you are still hungry, you may eat them. They are available to be eaten, but whether you chose to or not depends on other variables.

Soon enough, a promotion came my way, and with it, relocation across the country. We were transferred to Miami, Florida, where we hoped to buy a condo. We found a realtor and spent weeks searching for a place to live. We knew nothing about the real estate market, or what we needed to qualify for a mortgage. It didn't take long to realize that we had not been saving the money we needed to have a down payment to buy a house. We had to rent for the next few years.

Since we were making more money, we decided we could upgrade our lives. We found a great apartment overlooking the intercostal waterway and set up camp. Rent cost $1,700 for about 1,200 square feet. We bought our first living room and bedroom sets but had to use a loan from the furniture store to do it.

PER MONTH	
Net Paychecks	$ 4,000
Car Insurance	$ 150
Rent	$ 1,700
Car	$ 300
Utilities / Gas / Food	$ 600
Credit Card / Student Loans	$ 450
Money Available to Save (MATS)	$ 800

$3,200

$4,000 - $3,200 = $800

Two years later, I transferred again to southern California. Moving to California brought some shocking realities. First, the cost of living was nearly double that of Miami and Maui. We were making more money, but everything cost more. We were now paying $2,100 for a 1,200-square-foot apartment, higher income taxes, and more for basics like milk and gasoline. Soon, I became pregnant and had plenty of new things to spend money on. I obsessed over this little human. I bought every gadget, gimmick, and tool available. This period taught us a valuable life lesson: the amount of money we made stayed the same, but what we spent it on shifted. Since we were both working, daycare added a huge expense in addition to diapers.

PER MONTH	
Net Paychecks	$ 5,000
Car Insurance	$ 150
Rent	$ 2,100
Car	$ 300
Utilities / Gas / Food	$ 1,000
Credit Card / Student Loans	$ 550
Day Care	$ 600
Dipaers / Baby items	$ 200
Money Available to Save (MATS)	$ 100

$4,900

$5,000 - $4,900 = $100

The money that you have available to save will change over the course of your life. *When* you plan to have children will be a huge factor in these equations. Other factors like medical needs, the economy, and the job you chose will also have implications for what you can or cannot save. As you enter new chapters of life, be sure to always reevaluate your savings. Resist the urge to spend your whole paycheck in one day and risk spending the days after looking for coins. Becoming an Efficiency Bitch will require awareness and evaluation throughout your life.

Now that you know the money that you have available to save, let's talk about how to start controlling what you spend.

ALLOWANCE

One day, I looked at our credit card balance that had been climbing and decided we were not in a good place financially. We had lost sight of the money we were spending and how little we were saving as a result. We needed to get control of our spending, so I did some research and investigated how to save money. The irony makes me laugh because I had been a cost controller at a hotel for the better part of six years. I knew cost controls like the back of my hand, but somehow applying them to my personal life felt foreign to me.

When my mother-in-law (our kids call her Didi) came to town, I talked with her about budgets and money. I told her I'd been thinking about ways to budget and change our spending patterns. We wanted to save money to have a down payment on a house; what could we do to get there? Didi shared with me that in the past, she and my father-in-law (our kids call him Super-Papi) gave themselves a weekly allowance. They agreed to a specific allotment of money each week that they could spend on whatever they wanted. They shared all expenses for the family, house, and cars, and put away as much as they could in savings, but still wanted to have some play money. They each had total discretion on their allowance. If Super-Papi wanted to spend it on golf, he could. If Didi chose to save it and buy a new handbag at the end of the month, she could. Neither had nagging rights. This sounded like just the thing to get me and Steve moving. Now we were at a place where we could merge our money and set some ground rules. We needed a plan.

I spent my sixteen-week paid maternity leave (thanks to the state of California) reviewing our financials. I combed through our spending and determined what we had in extra income to save for a down payment on a house. I treated this exercise like a project at work. I checked every expense, sorted them into categories, and determined where we could trim the fat. I canceled subscriptions we didn't need, renegotiated utility bills like cable and Internet, and found areas where we were wasting money. I set up auto-drafts to a savings account as our "family play money" and gave us each a weekly allowance of $100. When we first landed on $100 a week, it seemed like a lot. Neither of us felt like we spent that much on non-essential items. We were both certain we would have some left over.

The following Sunday, I went to the ATM and pulled out $200 in twenties. I gave Steve his money and put mine in my wallet. I had no intention of changing any of my usual habits. I went about my days as I always did: manicure on Sunday, Starbucks every morning on the way to work, and soda from the vending machine at lunch. But something unexpected happened. I spent all my money by Thursday. I could not believe I had spent my allowance so quickly!

This started a new way of thinking for me that's lasted more than a decade and changed our family's financial position more than any income changes have. It's a mindset shift. We have a list for "Must Pay," "Might Buy," and "Want."

THE MUST PAY LIST

- rent/mortgage
- daycare
- utilities
- food
- insurance
- past debt (credit cards, student loans, car payments)

THE MIGHT BUY LIST

- manicure / pedicure
- Starbucks
- night out
- go to the movies
- new outfits for the baby

THE WANT LIST

- bigger television
- upgraded cell phone
- new golf clubs

As I got more into it, I developed a habit of tracking and reviewing where every penny went. I defined the Must Pay list as everything I was obligated to pay by contract or to live. My Might Buy list was everything I was used to buying at will but needed to think about before I indulged. My Want list was everything else I *wanted*. This list was important to me so that I could start to save the money I needed to afford the items I wanted, and not rely on a credit card to satisfy my wants.

By reviewing every cost, I could better distinguish the Want list from the Might Buy list. Soon, I stopped taking out cash and used our debit cards so we could track every penny, including our allowance. And by tracking every penny, we created a mindset shift both as individuals and as a family, which eventually resulted in us cutting down on our spending.

The habitual action of paying close attention to your spending provokes a mindset shift, which in turn helps you reach your saving and money goals. By paying more attention, you become more efficient with your money. Huzzah!

By the end of the first year of this process, we had enough money saved to put a down payment on a Federal Housing Administration (FHA) loan. Different types of mortgages are available to people based on credit, cash, veteran status, etc. An FHA loan allows for a low-down payment but includes the cost of Private Mortgage Insurance (PMI). This is an amount added to your monthly mortgage payment to protect the bank if you stop paying. This is an excellent option for a first-time homebuyer—but if you use it, watch the market. If your home increases in value in one to two years, you may be able to refinance and get rid of the PMI. This will save you quite a bit of money in the long run. When we refinanced our home and dropped the PMI, we were able to save about a hundred dollars a month. Mortgages and home buying are complex processes. I have bought and sold three homes in my life, and I have learned something every time. Plus, the market changes, the laws change, and what banks are willing to lend changes. My best advice for any home buyer is to interview your agent and mortgage lender. Find someone who is not only experienced but willing to educate you in the process.

CALCULATE YOUR MONEY AVAILABLE TO SPEND (MATS)

Okay, back to the Money Available to Spend. MATS is the key to financial freedom. Your money will not save itself; time for you to take control. Do you know what your MATS is? Try this simple exercise. Don't make it too compli-cated. We're just looking for a general idea here.

First, decide if you are an employee or a contractor. An employee has tax-es deducted from their paycheck and receives a W2 at the end of the year. A contractor does not have taxes taken out and receives a 1099-NEC at the end of the year.

If you are a small business owner, you will receive a Schedule C from your business.

If you are an employee:

1. Determine your net paycheck, which is your gross pay less tax and oth-er withholdings (often the amount that hits your bank account). If your paycheck amount is variable, take a reasonable estimate.
2. Multiply the net pay by how many checks you receive in one year, then divide by twelve. Now you know the average amount of money that enters your bank account each month.

Pay period cycles are typically weekly (fifty-two times a year), bi-weekly (every other week—twenty-six times a year), bi-monthly (twice a month—twenty-four times a year), or monthly (once a month—twelve times a year).

3. List every expense that you are obligated to pay; these are the items that are on your "Must Pay" list.

If you are an independent contractor or a small business owner (receiv-ing a 1099-NEC or Schedule C), do everything the same as above but also be sure to include 20-25 percent of your total pay for taxes since they have not been accounted for.

4. Finally, add up all your expenses. Money In – Money Out = MATS

If this number is negative, you are already over-committed, and we have work to do. We'll get to that later in this chapter.

If you have a positive number, this is your Money Available to Save. This is the extra money you have—the fries at the bottom of the bag. Now, let's decide what to eat (spend) and what to leave (save).

The cold, hard truth is if you don't have a plan, the money will likely get spent on something you don't even remember buying. Money can disappear if you are not paying close attention. So, let's put a manageable plan in place. Then, you can tweak it to be more or less complex, depending on where you are in your personal finance journey.

WEALTH MANAGEMENT

I've been working with money since age sixteen. I'd consider myself an expert, but I surely don't know everything. Once I learned how to save money, I needed help learning how to build wealth for the future. I'm not talking about how to become a millionaire. I'm talking about having financial comfort and discipline to save money for various parts of life. I don't want my future self to panic about being able to afford a replacement water heater, and I definitely want to retire comfortably.

Five years after my mindset shift on spending, we hired my family's first wealth manager. We had started down the savings path and had reached a point where we had momentum. We were ready to learn how to really grow our money for our future.

In all honestly, her title intimidated me. I thought, "Will she laugh at us when she finds out how much wealth we *don't* have?" But we did it anyway. We knew we needed professional help to get on the right track. The first thing she taught us was to think of money goals like four pockets in your pants.

The first pocket is for your committed expenses. We defined that in the last section. This money should be in your checking account. Your paycheck should direct deposit here and expenses are deducted from the same account. This account is Money In, Money Out.

Here is where the fun starts. All the other pockets contain money from MATS. We are going to fill your other three pockets with savings so that you never have to panic about money again.

The second pocket is your emergency fund. This is the money that you keep locked up tight in case of, you guessed it, an emergency. An emergency is not deciding you want a new outfit or to go skiing this weekend. An emergency is putting tires on your car, replacing your water heater, or covering expenses when you lose your job and have no income for two months.

The amount you need to save depends on the spending commitments in your first pocket; on a conservative level, I would shoot for one-and-a-half times your committed expenses or your Must Pay List. Others will tell you to have a six-month supply. If you're starting from zero, go with $1,000 as a target, celebrate, and build from there. You will want to meet this target first before moving on to fill the other two pockets.

As an example, if your Must Pay total (from your first pocket) is $2,500, your initial target x1.5 is $3,750. Once you hit it, you can start moving to the third and fourth pockets. Continue to add to the emergency fund by keeping a smaller flow of cash moving into this pocket as you add larger amounts into pockets three and four. Consider $25-$50 a week. The balance will grow quickly and allow you the flexibility to make withdrawals or adjustments in the case of an emergency.

Ideally, this money should be in a separate bank account but not easily accessed. I have mine in a savings account at the same bank where I hold my checking. I turn off ATM access and online banking. I can only access it by going into the bank. When choosing a savings account type, select one where you will not incur fees. Most of these are based on daily or monthly minimum balances.

After you have your emergency fund, it's time to work on the near-term savings account. This will be your third pocket. Think of a vacation, a down payment for a house or car, or a new living room couch. This is money you've earmarked for a specific purchase. It's there so that when you are ready to make that big purchase one to three years from now, you can whip out a sack of cash rather than sign up for a credit card with thirty percent interest rate. At first, I had this money in the same savings account as my second pocket. However, I eventually moved it to a separate account. If you have a wealth manager, explain the goals of this money. Ask them about setting it up in an investment account that is easily accessible but can earn interest while it waits. Opening another savings account will be fine; it just won't earn much interest. As your money grows, you'll want to expand this pocket with the "extra" you have.

The fourth pocket is for longer-term savings. Although these things are far into the future, they need to be actioned today. For many people, this includes retirement, sending kids to college, and long-term healthcare. The U.S. government wants us to save for these things too. The government encourages us to do so by making tax deferred accounts especially for them. A 401(k) and an Individual Retirement Account (IRA) are the most popular. A 401(k) is a retirement account that an employer offers as a benefit to its employees. The money is deducted from your paycheck before tax (this is important) and put into an account you cannot touch until you are fifty-nine and a half years old. After leaving your employer, the money belongs to you and grows through compounding interest for years. Some employers offer a match program to encourage retirement savings. If yours does, contribute enough to get the match; it's literally free money. After you meet the match, work towards maximum contribution (a limit set by the IRS every year) by increasing one percent every year. The benefit of adding one percent every year is that it will grow your savings quickly without impacting your lifestyle.

An IRA is an account that anyone can set up and helps reduce taxable liability while building a retirement savings account. There are many types of IRAs so be sure to discuss with a Wealth Manager to find the one that works best for you.

A Health Savings Account (HSA) is another excellent way to set aside savings for future you. You will have health expenses in the future; that's a fact of life. Money in an HSA is typically pulled from your paycheck. The money is pretax, grows tax-free, and is yours for life. The trick here is to treat it as a savings account. Let's say you contribute $1,000 to this account this year. Then you have a $200 medical bill. If you can afford to pay some or all of the medical bill via your first two pockets, do so, and leave the money in the HSA to grow and earn interest. The IRS sets a maximum that you can contribute to this account every year. Contribute as much as you can today and increase it one percent every year. Work towards a goal of maxing it out.

A 529 college savings plan is another U.S. government incentive to save for education. This account can be used for kindergarten through twelfth grade, as well as trade school and university. The account beneficiary can be changed as needed, so it will benefit your future self, spouse, or children who will eventually need education. Talk to a financial advisor about how much to add here. The account will grow tax-free but is added after-tax deductions. It's a great way to build savings for future education expenses.

It's important to note that tax deferred savings accounts like a 401(k), 529-plan, Health Savings Accounts, and IRA all have penalties for pulling money out early or for reasons not covered by the plan. Once the money is set aside for these reasons, do everything you can to never count on them. Paying these penalties will cost you significantly.

Getting all this set up will take some effort, but I promise you it's worth it. Here's a quick recap of the action steps you can take to get started:

1. Set up a savings account at the same bank where you have a checking account. Start adding to your emergency fund.
2. Ask your employer if they offer a 401(k) plan. If you are eligible to contribute, start today. I always recommend three percent to start and challenge yourself to increase one percent every six months. If not, make a note in your calendar of when you can (every plan is different). If you're your employer does not offer a 401(k) or you are self-employed, don't get discouraged. Talk to a finance professional or bank about opening an Independent Retirement Account (IRA).
3. Ask your employer about an HSA account. Do they offer it, and how can you set that up? Take note of the date and do your research ahead of time. Note that this is not the same as a Flexible Spending Account (FSA). With an FSA, you use it or lose it.
4. Visit your payroll department. Tell them you want one to five percent of your paycheck directly deposited into your savings account (from step 1). If your employer does not offer this or you are self-employed you can set up auto draft at the bank.

The goal is to automate your savings process so that you don't have to think about it. Get it started, no matter how small. Make a note in your calendar six months from now to review these percentages and increase them by one percent. Your balance will grow fast over time. After completing this, add these amounts to your budget line items and deduct from your MATS calculations as described in the prior section. Review this process at least once a year.

ON THE ROAD TO FINANCIAL FREEDOM

So now your pants are full of money, and I hope it's not burning a hole in your pockets. You know what your MATS is and how to separate the money into categories for your current life, emergency, short-term, and long-term savings. Now let's look at how to improve that MATS number, which will add money to your third and fourth pockets.

For this, I'll use an analogy that Didi came up with. Think of money management the way you drive a car. You get in the car and turn the key. When you drive, you have a destination in mind, a place where you are headed. In money management, you have goals. You put the car in Drive and hit the gas gently. This is you making the allocations to your various savings accounts: emergency fund, short-term savings account, 401(k), and HSA. Check.

You pick up speed. Where are you looking? Likely out the front windshield most of the time. Is there anything on the road? Pedestrians, other cars, kids on bikes? In money management, these will be life events that can cost or earn you extra money. For example, a holiday where you need to spend more than your monthly allotment on gifts. Which account will you pull it from? Think ahead and give yourself a cap. Another example is getting a cash gift or a bonus from work. Again, think ahead about which pocket you will put this in. Think about these items now and write them down in a list.

Soon, you are on the main road and need to look farther ahead. When is the next traffic light? Any major traffic jams coming up? Think a little farther down the road about what you might encounter. Do you have a wedding to attend next year? Do you have a large payment due for insurance or tuition? Add them to your list. Which pocket will they pull from?

I would advise you not to consider a tax refund in this area. I know many people who count on their tax refund to pay off debt or fund an emergency.

If you receive a large tax refund every year, you'll need to correct the amount of withholding from your paycheck. There are multiple philosophies on tax withholding, but I'm a firm believer in paying what I owe—nothing more, nothing less. You are in the right range if you get a refund of $300-$500 per year. Anything more than that and you're giving the government a free loan. If you owe money, you'll need to increase your tax withholding elections and potentially pay quarterly taxes to avoid this, especially if you are an independent contractor or business owner. When in doubt, find a Certified Public Accountant (CPA) who can help you understand the best approach for your personal tax situation. Taxes are complicated, and the more money you make, the more complicated it will become. When shopping for a CPA, do your research and ask friends you trust for referrals. People often ask me how do pick a good CPA. My advice is to find one who asks you a lot of questions and wants to learn about your situation. Any CPA can enter data into tax forms, the good ones do so with your tax situation in mind.

Of course, while driving, we don't just stare straight in front of us. We check our rearview mirror frequently. The same goes for money management. Develop a habit of looking at the money you've spent every month. This will give you a clear picture of what you spend and what you waste. As an accounting professional, I keep a Profit and Loss Statement for my household. It may seem silly to some, but it's the view I'm the most familiar with, so it works for me. You may need something in a different format. You can start with software programs like You Need a Budget, Quicken, and Mint. Or tools like Rocket Money may work better. New tools are always coming on the market, so research and find one that works for you. Your bank may even have this feature. With some banks, you can tag a transaction and create reports to download. One of my favorite ways is to download all the transactions from my credit card and checking account into a CSV file. Then, I sort all the transactions into Excel or Numbers. If you try this, you can categorize your transactions in as much or as little detail as you like.

I tracked my family's spending for six months and drilled down on the fast-food expenses. It's shocking to see the number associated with a twice-a-week drive-through habit. I set a goal to reduce it. Just seeing the number helped curb it. Over the next six months, I reduced the amount from $1,000 per month to less than $100. I included my kids in the monthly review and excitement when we met our goal.

Another example that I do with my kids is tracking how much money we spend on ice cream. Now, before you judge our consumption of empty calories smothered in sugar, remember we live in Arizona and it's freaking hot here. Plus, ice cream is good. We love ice cream, and we spend a lot of money proving it. But it was getting out of control, and I had to put a stop to the madness.

I started pulling the transactions from our bank statements and searching for our usual ice cream stops. By doing this, I was able to easily show the kids just how much money we spent on these special treats. I'm careful not to use the word "waste" when I talk about this money. I don't think we are wasting it; we enjoy it. But I do think it's important to know the hard numbers and have a target in mind to decide when we have hit the monthly limit. After this realization that we were overindulging, as a family, we decided on the max amount we would spend in a month. It's something we can track and take responsibility for, without creating stress or a scarcity mindset.

Think about the areas you spend extra money on because they are things that you enjoy. Can you cap some of these? Some common ones among women I work with are daily $7.00 coffee, manicures, pedicures, eyelash extensions, and tattoos. I'm not suggesting you stop these things all together, everyone deserves a little pampering. But to get clarity on your finance you need to get a solid understanding of just how much you are spending on these items in order to curb them.

To make these types of cuts, limit the amount of cash you keep on hand. Cash is harder to track. Some people tell me they are better with cash, and while that may be true, you need to learn to be good with plastic cards too. Some places don't take cash anymore because it requires extra work to balance cashier tills and occasionally results in theft. Famous personal financial radio personality Dave Ramsey has built an empire around the use of cash and envelopes to budget and control costs. Older generations often say keeping cash helps them control their money better. While there is some value to the concepts around cash, I believe they are outdated. Generations responsible for this mindset used checks that took weeks to clear the bank, not debit and credit card charges that get posted immediately. You can see a snapshot of what's in your account at any moment if you stick to electronic payments. Similarly, limit checks as much as possible. Writing checks creates a float period where you need to be more aware of the payments you promised but have not yet accounted for. If you write a check for $300 and the person cashes it six months later (which they are allowed to do), you may have forgotten about it.

The last part of the car analogy is your peripheral vision, knowing what's going on around you. You must look side to side as you turn or approach an intersection. The same goes for money management. The stock market, inflation, world events (like global pandemics, government elections and war), and tax changes are the sidelines of money management. You don't need to spend a lot of time worrying about them, but you need to be aware of them. Glance over from time to time; see what's going on around you. You may find things that can help you grow and a reason to tap the brakes on a part of your plan.

CREDIT CARDS AND CREDIT SCORES

We can't have a chapter on money without talking about the giant, hairy, drooling monster in the room: credit cards. Credit cards are one of the great necessary evils; if you don't know how tame this beast, it will bite your head off.

Credit cards are designed to cost you a lot of money. Credit card companies make money by you not being able to afford something now and wanting or needing it. They offer discounts to sign up, free airline tickets, or cash back, but then the fees come in like a tidal wave: annual fees, late fees, growing and changing interest rates. Not to mention, when you use your credit card at a store, they charge the store a three to four percent fee on top of that. They are making money *everywhere*. Do not fall for their antics. Another little clever trick that credit card companies use is sending you a "convenience check" in the mail. They lure you in, claiming to defer payments for months. The trick is they compound the interest and hit you with it all at once later. I personally know more than one person who has accumulated crippling debt using this "convenience check" that their credit card company so graciously offered.

Now that you know all the pitfalls of credit cards, let's talk about how to live in their world. They exist, and you can't ignore them. If you're not careful, though, you'll find they can not only get into your pockets, but also eat all your money, the pants themselves, and pick their teeth with the zipper.

Only use credit cards that offer no annual fee. Look for cards that offer perks that you are interested in. I have two credit cards, one at my main bank that offers cash back and one from an airline that offers significant travel perks like companion passes, lounge access, and free checked baggage. Don't spend money on a credit card that you cannot pay off right away. In fact, one thing I do is set up automatic payment of the full balance each month. By paying off the card in full each month, you avoid interest, improve your credit score, and earn the perks. The credit card is used to earn a benefit and not build a balance. Don't be lulled into the idea that you only have to make the minimum payments. You will end up paying three times more than the item cost and take years to get there. If you choose to use credit cards, use extra caution and discipline. If you can do it, you can beat the system and find the benefits many seek.

A credit card is often the first lending product a person applies for in life. Other lines of credit may include a car loan, home mortgage, or personal loan. To get credit, you have to apply, providing a variety of personal information. The bank runs your credit rating using one or more of three credit reporting bureaus. In the U.S., as of 2022, they are TransUnion, Experian, and Equifax. Their job is to collect data on each social security number and provide a rating based on how well or poorly an applicant spends money. You may hear a credit score referred to as a FICO score. FICO is a data analytics company that analyzes data from the three bureaus and produces a combined score. According to Experian,[13] five main factors weight your score:

1. **Your payment history:** Do you pay your bills on time? Accounts that impact your payment history are those you have used your social

security number to obtain. Think cell phone, electricity, rent, and water bill. These companies run your credit when you set up a service. Your credit score will be negatively impacted if you pay your bills late. This counts for around thirty-five percent of your credit score.

2. **Amount owed:** How much money do you owe to other lenders? A lender wants to know when they will be paid if they give you money. If you owe money to other lenders, your prospective lender may be near the back of the line to get paid. The fewer lenders you have (the shorter the line), the better your score will be. This accounts for about thirty percent of your score.

3. **Length of history:** How long have you had credit established? When you start out, you automatically have a low credit score. It's challenging to get credit when you don't have credit. In this case, the lenders who give credit often have very high interest rates and fees because they are taking a gamble on an unknown credit user. One way to avoid this is to find another person with great credit and have them co-sign with you. Be very careful and thoughtful when you do this. If that person has good credit and they are willing to vouch for you, you inherit some of that good credit score mojo. But if you mess up, it will impact them, so take this seriously. Conversely, bad credit can attach itself to you too. If your co-signer has bad credit, you get some of that reputation. Be extra cautious both as the co-signer and co-signee. This category accounts for about fifteen percent of your credit score.

4. **New credit inquiries:** If you are desperate for credit and apply to multiple lenders simultaneously, your credit score will be negatively impacted. Opening several accounts around the same time is a big no-no. It alerts the bank that if you were not in debt, you could very well be soon. Be strategic when opening credit accounts. Don't apply for every retail credit card because of the shiny discounts they offer. That's a fast track to lowering your score. This accounts for about ten percent of your credit score.

5. **Types of credit used:** You will need a diverse set of credit accounts in your record to have a perfect credit score. A car loan and a credit

card diversify your credit report and can increase your score. Again, do this thoughtfully. Don't take a ten percent interest rate car loan if you have the cash to pay for it simply to diversify your score. This can be hard to do when you are first building credit, but as life happens, you will obtain credit in more diverse ways. This accounts for about ten percent of your credit score.

When you apply to rent an apartment, the landlord or management office will run your credit report. If you have past due utility bills or owe rent to another landlord, they may choose not to rent to you, charge you more, or request a down payment. The better your credit score, the better your buying power in everything from renting an apartment to car loans to a home mortgage. The system rewards those who use credit wisely and hinders those who do not.

Now that you know what impacts your credit score, you need to know how to check it. I recommend you check your credit score once a year. I have a repeat entry in my calendar on January first to check my credit score. Checking your score more than once a year may damage your score, so don't get excited and check it once a week. Checking your own score is known as a "soft check." When a lender or creditor runs your report, it's a "hard check." It indicates you are inquiring about getting more credit. This lowers your score under number two, above, as it assumes you want to borrow more.

There are many ways to check your score. In 2022, the big ones are Credit Karma and FreeCreditReport.com. Read the fine print on these services as they will sell you a monthly subscription to credit monitoring, which you probably don't need. Uncheck the box (they cleverly default to sign up), get your score, and move on. Credit scores range from 300 to 850. Typically, anything under 629 is considered a bad score. 630-689 is fair, 690-719 is good, and 720-850 is excellent. The higher your score, the lower interest rate you will pay and the more "buying power" you will have.

Earlier this year, I bought a new car. Alone at the dealership, I found the car I wanted and negotiated the price. Once we settled on the price, the time came for financing. The man asked me if I had a co-signer to apply with me.

"No," I said. "Just me."

He asked if I had a down payment in addition to my trade-in.

"Nope, just the trade-in."

I could sense concern, but I didn't know why. I signed all the forms, and he ran my credit report. My score came back 810. He looked at me and smiled. He said, "I'm sorry if I made you uncomfortable. I don't get many women here who can qualify for a loan by themselves. With this score, I'll write you a loan for two cars."

Ladies, we must change this. I can't be the anomaly of women and great credit scores. When I thought about this more, I realized women in the U.S. have only been able to apply for credit beginning in 1974 with the Fair Lending Act. My own mother was a police officer in Tucson, Arizona, and still couldn't get a credit card without her father or husband co-signing. Even though not many generations of women have learned to pass down best practices, it's our responsibility to learn about credit, improve it, and teach it to others. If you can find a local class or lecture on credit score education or improvement tactics, I highly encourage you to do so.

Now the big question: What's your credit score? If it's been more than twelve months since you ran your credit report, run it today. Get an idea of what is on your credit report. Close credit cards that you do not use. Find out if anyone has sent you to collections. And, of course, check for fraud. Don't worry if these numbers are not great today. Everyone starts somewhere. You can move it forward; it's not complicated, but it does take deliberate steps to get there. Step one is knowing where you are starting.

NEW GENERATIONS, NEW IDEAS

Another interesting area to consider for wealth management is the Financial Independence, Retire Early (FIRE) movement. It's a lifestyle that ignited in the 2010s by millennials who wanted to maximize savings early in life to avoid working forever. The objective is to accumulate assets until the passive income provides enough money to live without a paying job. This concept is achieved through aggressive savings up to fifty percent of your total income. It's a big goal, but if you're reading this book in the early chapters of your life, it may be the best thing you ever did for your future self. Here are some of the basic concepts presented by FIRE:

- At a savings rate of ten percent, it takes nine years of work to save for one year of living expenses.
- At a savings rate of 25 percent, it takes three years of work to save for one year of living expenses.
- At a savings rate of 50 percent, it takes one year of work to save for one year of living expenses.
- At a savings rate of 75 percent, it takes 1/3 year (four months) of work to save for one year of living expenses.

Learning or unlearning about money can be uncomfortable. Take your time. Give yourself space to work through the lessons accumulated over your life. Work through some of your beliefs about money and get ready to leap into a new mindset. Talk to your partner, parents, and friends. Warning: not everyone will be willing to talk about money. Find someone who will. If you can't find anyone, email me. I love to talk about money!

Ask an older person something about money. Use the opportunity to start a dialogue. And of course, don't forget to pay it forward. Start a conversation about money with a person younger than you. Teach them something you know. If you are a parent, please talk to your kids about money. Even if it's just to say, "I don't know a lot about money, but I'm going to learn."

According to the American Psychological Association, money is the number one cause of stress.[14] Stress is the number one cause of obesity, lack of sleep, and depression. Learn about money now any way you can. No matter how you started, no matter your education (or lack thereof), learning about money *now* will help you forever. Yes, it can be hard to recover; you may have some work cut out for you, but you can do this.

When parents stress over money, they create stress in children. In fact, children who hear their parents fight or speak negatively about money are more likely to get into debt within the first years of leaving their parents' home. In addition, parents who stress about money are more likely to get divorced than for any other reason.[15] You don't have to be a finance expert or debt-free to teach your children smart money management. All you need is the desire for them to have a financially independent life and the willingness to discuss. Talking to your kids about the financial decisions you are making today and mistakes you've made in the past will stick with them throughout their lives. Kids pay attention and absorb what you say (and don't say) about money.

Our seven-year-old son loves to collect coins. He finds them around the house, on the street, and asks his grandparents for their spare change. One day he brought me his hand-painted wooden box and offered it to me to help pay for the house. I considered my response. I could tell him, "No, thank you. You keep it." Or I could accept his $2.37 contribution. After a few seconds, I said, "That is very thoughtful of you. I'm so proud of you for saving your money and offering to contribute to buying our new house. How about we do this: let's split it into three parts. You contribute part to pay for the house, you keep part of the spending for a new toy for the new house, and you save part to spend after we move in."

He loved this idea. He spent twenty minutes deciding how much to put in each category. He ended up giving me fifty cents for the house. He kept one dollar for the toy for the new house, and saved the rest for after we moved in. I took him to the dollar store that very day and let him pick out his new toy. This example illustrates that his understanding of money's value is evolving even at the age of seven. Although he may not understand the overall value of the house and the mortgage payment that comes with it, he does know that he has currency with a present and future value.

A final thought as we conclude our chapter about money. The shame, stress, and embarrassment that can exist for some around not having money can also be present for those who have it. I have firsthand stories from women who have felt that they can't celebrate their financial success for fear of being seen as bragging. While money, or the lack thereof, does not define your character or work ethic, it can profoundly impact your confidence—and fear of judgement. As you work through your relationship with money, take time to reflect on the full spectrum of the way you experience money. Celebrate your success and milestones along the way. If you need someone to celebrate with you, email me any time. I will cheer for you, from the first dollar saved to the million-dollar mark and everything in between.

As much as I love talking about personal finance, I really shine with small businesses. If you own a small business, please reach out to me at **Info@TwoSenseConsulting.com.**

> *"I was married in my early thirties and had children in the years that followed. Waiting to start a family gave me the opportunity to finish college and begin a career path that I absolutely love. I am happy and comfortable in my career and know that I am capable of financially and mentally taking care of my family."*

Melinda Dickinson, mother of two
Director, Culture and Training, Hensley Beverage Company

CHAPTER 3
I for **INBOX**

My dad once told me, "Life requires maintenance."

These words have stayed with me for a long time. They remind me that the inbox of life will never be empty. Everything needs work and will need work again after you have done it. This goes for your home, email inbox, car maintenance, grocery list, and inbox at school or work. It doesn't matter how much you do today, there will always be more to do tomorrow. It's a sobering thought. No matter how hard we work, we will always have more to do. But this motivates me to get things done faster and wiser every day. It allows me clarity, opening up time to relax and play, while also allowing me time to make my dreams come true and live the best life possible. That's what this chapter is all about.

Whenever I finish a project, I take on three more. I love to be part of things. I love to learn and meet new people. I accepted appointment as my sorority's pledge class president in college, and I volunteered to coach a youth softball team long before I had kids. I volunteered to be a Girl Scout troop leader and the Communications Chair for the Project Management Institute. I agreed to be the Parent Teacher Organization (PTO) president for two years and kindergarten room mom. I joined committees and side projects at work and said yes to just about everything.

I sign up for everything under the sun not because I'm padding my resume, but because I genuinely enjoy being active in groups. Being part of everything, however, creates more and more inboxes to manage, lists to develop, and tasks to get done. There's a very delicate harmony and priority to it all. I have not always been good at saying no, but today I'm very deliberate about what groups I join and volunteer for, but you'll have to wait until the C for Connection chapter to hear more of that.

Life is not a competition to see who is the busiest, despite often feeling that way in modern society. I've made it my mission to manage my inbox (and my time) in a way that will allow me to do all the things I love. Not every one of my tips will work for you, and none of them will work forever.

I want a challenge—but I'm not superhuman. I get overstimulated and overworked just like everyone else. I pride myself on always looking for a way to save time, energy, and money in the long run.

All the tasks you are about to read are the basics of how I do life. They shape my mentality and motivation. I am always coming up with new ways to spend less time on my inbox while ensuring I never miss a task or have to duplicate work. Nothing is more embarrassing than saying I will do something and then not getting it done, being late, or completing something that's only half-baked.

This chapter will teach you practical ways to manage the inboxes of your life. Being an Efficiency Bitch means managing things in the most streamlined and effective manner possible.

TOUCH IT ONCE

Everything you do, and I mean everything, plan to touch once and never again. When you get the mail, open and sort it immediately. If you are cleaning the house, get all the dirty clothes together and start a load of laundry right then. If you take your shoes off when you enter the door, put a basket at the door to collect them. It's a simple concept that changes your inbox volume immediately. Hold your kids accountable to it. Every day when they enter the house, they must hang up their backpacks and put their lunchboxes in the kitchen. It's easier to take care of it the first time than having to go find it later, wasting precious time on the search.

Do your best to avoid opening an email that you can't respond to right away. When it does happen, mark the email "unread" or put a note on your desk office so you don't forget. Delete emails that you do not need and file emails that are complete. Your "inbox" of email should only be for items that you still need to action.

Treat your text messages the same way. Review text messages to ensure everything is responded to or completed. Delete the ones that are complete. If there is something that needs to get completed or a message needs a response, leave it. Once completed or replied to, delete it. If you have a hard time thinking about losing your text messages history forever, you can save them to the cloud for historic filing while maintaining a clean "inbox" on your phone.

NEVER RELY ON MEMORY

Your memory will disappoint you more often than impress you. The more you add to your plate, and the older you get, the higher the chance you will forget something. Make a promise to yourself right now that you will stop relying on memory and begin a habit of writing things down. If you don't have paper, text message yourself so you won't forget. Use sticky notes and whiteboards to remind yourself of important items.

Being the "Time Keeper" is an exhausting mental inbox to keep clean. Smartphones have great alarm features where you can set repeating alarms, label them and prepare ahead. I have one to remind myself to pick up the kids after school and take them to piano lessons. I have another alarm to remind me to record my podcast. With all the things happening around an EB, it's easy to show up late to a meeting or school pickup, something the original EB has strong feelings about.

My mom, the original EB, has an allergic reaction to being late. "Hate" is not a strong enough word to explain her discomfort with being late and I certainly inherited this visceral reaction. We recognize how important every minute is and refuse to cost other people precious minutes because I relied on my memory and arrived ten minutes late.

I'm not late often, but if I am, it's because I either forgot to set an alarm, or I was multi-tasking when I should not have been. There is a time and a place for multi-tasking—like brushing your teeth and picking out what to wear for the day. But the overuse of multi-tasking will result in poor performance, repeated tasks, and running late. Be present during the task at hand, write down the other item so you don't forget, or schedule it in your calendar for later.

"Beware of multitasking. Just because you can do
two things at once does not mean you should."
Christina Fell, mother of three
Bank Executive

Checklists, checklists, checklists. They help me keep my life in order. I have them all over the place for different things at different times. I have a work to-do list, a grocery list (using Amazon Alexa), a household chore list for daily tasks and ongoing projects. I have a Christmas gift list, a birthday party checklist, and an onboarding checklist for clients. The point is if I do a task on repeat, I prepare a checklist, so I don't forget a step. If it's a one-off item, I add it to a "to-do" checklist, so I won't forget. And the best part of writing a checklist is *crossing it off the list.* Don't deprive yourself of this satisfaction. There is real data that shows the feel-good hormones we get from taking this simple step. You deserve that feeling. Go ahead, write it down just so you can cross it off. I do it all the time.

EMBRACE IMPERFECT ACTION

I am far from a perfectionist. What I am, though, is a taskmaster. I attempt to do something quickly and see if it sticks rather than spend hours trying to make something work. My husband is a perfectionist. If he is going to do something, it will be done the first time perfectly. We tease each other about the best approach, but they both serve a purpose. It makes no sense to be a perfectionist when putting kids' clothes away because they will destroy them an hour later. Likewise, it makes no sense to install motion-sensor lights quick and dirty because they probably won't work. Most of the things I touch require imperfect action. When it's needed, I call in the perfectionist.

I have gotten good at asking people I trust to help me make these decisions. For example, let's say we want a new dining room table. I do some online shopping. I send links of three or four items I like to Steve. He looks at them and makes the final decision. If I don't separate the preliminary decision from the final decision, I get stuck in analysis paralysis, and nothing ever happens. We followed this process when buying a house and a car, selecting a wedding venue, and choosing baby names. If you're good at the final decision but tend to choose too quickly, let someone else do the upfront research to ensure you get the best options available.

> "*Be flexible, with both your personal and professional expectations.*
> *Things are much messier than you expect, but also more joyful!*"
>
> **Kim Cole, mother of three**
> **Director of Public Relations**

USE TECHNOLOGY

Today, some of my favorite technologies are my Amazon Alexa, Apple Watch, and iPhone. They've been around for a while, but they're always being updated. I like that each automates small things in my life so that I don't have to think about them. When you invest in a tool like this, use it to its full potential. You can search YouTube for videos on the best ways to use Amazon Alexa, for example. You will be shocked at some of the things it can do that are not common knowledge. Using it only for playing music and a grocery list is like driving a Porsche around the neighborhood. My favorite of these devices is my Apple Watch. I wear it twenty-three hours a day. I use it to track my sleep, exercise, menstrual cycle, calendar, and so much more. I use the "Infograph Modular" watch face. It's my favorite because I can choose which apps to see on the screen face. I customized mine to view unread text messages with the date and time across the top. In the middle, my calendar shows the next appointment with the workout tracker, my cycle tracker, and the current weather forecast along the bottom. I could not function as efficiently without it.

Check your email. I check my email four times a day. Early morning, I look for new meetings, but do not read each email. Around 10:00 a.m. and 3:00 p.m., I answer emails. At 8:00 p.m., I look for the next day's meetings. I unsubscribe from mailing lists. As I mentioned before, I delete all the emails I no longer need and file ones that I need to keep for reference later. Only emails that require action remain in my inbox. If my inbox gets longer than five to eight emails, I need to schedule a little longer to resolve them. I'll carve out some time in my calendar to resolve and action the open requests, whether they are personal or business.

I have three email addresses that created three separate calendars for me, all of which I can access from my phone and my Apple Watch:

1. **Work:** all work-related communication, meetings, and events. Color coded in red.

2. **Personal:** All items that pertain only to me, like doctor appointments, haircuts, etc. Color coded in purple.

3. **Family:** All items that pertain to the house, the dog, or the kids. My husband and I share this inbox and calendar. Color coded in green.

Life is one big inbox. If tasks don't get added to the calendar, they may be late or never get done. As ambitious women we know life is busy, we like it that way. Managing jobs, sports, school, homework, errands, doctor appointments, and everything else, it can be easy to lose track of who is doing what and when.

Google Calendar has become my go-to solution to pull all my inboxes into one app. I find its layout the most user-friendly and easy to work with in a shared space. It's compatible with Yahoo, Outlook, Hotmail and more. Color codes listed above show on the calendar, so it's obvious instantly where the tasks of the day will be. You can easily add one time or ongoing reminders and tasks that must be marked complete or moved forward to the next day. My husband has access to and maintains the family email and calendar as much as I do. We sync it to the Amazon Alexa Show so the kids can also see the family calendar at a glance. The whole family knows when the events are occurring, including family members birthdays.

If you have not met Amazon Alexa, allow me to introduce you. An Amazon Echo is a smart speaker, an Amazon Echo Show is a smart speaker with a built-in monitor, and they both have a voice-activated virtual assistant called Alexa. Alexa can manage dozens of commands: "set a timer," "create a list," "search the Internet," "tell me a joke," "call a friend," "set up routines," and more. They can be used as intercoms when connected to each other and can play music throughout the house. There are a variety of smart speakers and virtual assistants available on the market, but as of the publication date of this book, I believe "Alexa" has the best functionality and the most intuitive set-up.

Living with robots. Anything that reduces my need to think about something is a win in my book. A few years ago, my husband had the brilliant idea of installing motion-sensor lights in our kitchen pantry. Initially, we wanted to reduce electricity usage since kids always leave lights on. But these lights turned out to be one of the best mental inbox life hacks. Now we have motion-sensor lights in our closets, pantry, laundry room, and garage. We no longer wonder if the lights were left on all day or try to balance a full load of groceries in our arms while also reaching for the light switch as we enter the house. Little things like this go a long way in the general cleanliness of your mental inbox. To take it to another level, I suggest automated timers on exterior lights, interior lights, and holiday decorations. Once these are all set up you can program your Amazon Alexa to turn lights on or off on command. It's the little things that can make a huge difference.

In addition to Amazon Alexa, my other favorite robot is Roomba. This magical little robot vacuums up all the crumbs, dirt, and hair off our floors. It is programmed to run daily at 10:00 a.m. They are expensive, and the knock-offs don't work well in my experience, but it's one of the top five investments I've ever made. With a home full of kids and the cutest puppy you will ever see, this amazing robot cleans my house every day without being asked once. They are available refurbished, which can often help with the cost. This will make your life better the first time you use it, so consider a savings plan in your third pant pocket just for this (refer to the Bank chapter for a refresh). The new versions are compatible with Alexa. So for a real automated experience, try, "Alexa, tell the Roomba to clean the house." It's both hysterical and awesome.

We received the Nest Smart Home Thermostat as a Christmas gift one year. Before I had one, I didn't see the value. Now I highly recommend it to everyone. We live in Arizona, so when it's hot, it's stupid hot. The electric bill can cost more than $500 in the summer months. We love this thermostat because it gets smarter over time and keeps the house at the temperature we want without having to take any action. On eco mode, the temperature control uses as little energy as possible. We can modify the thermostat when we are away to turn the air conditioning off or turn it back on to cool the house before our arrival. And guess what else? You guessed it. It also connects to Alexa.

Auto-ship. I set up automatic shipping for many items that I know I need but will easily forget. For example, it's dusty in Arizona, and we use the Air Conditioning damn near year-round. Because of this, we have to replace the air filters about every two months. I don't want to use precious brain power trying to remember this. Instead, I created an auto-ship on Amazon to deliver them every other month. When they show up, out with the old, in with the new. Done and done. I have everything from air filters to vitamins and protein powder on auto-ship. When my kids were little, I had diapers and wipes on the list. Amazon is a great place to look for auto-ship items, but you can find many sites that offer it. If you choose auto-ship, be sure you are using the items and not ending up with a stockpile. Only keep things on auto-ship that you use regularly. It makes no sense to have a product on auto-ship and not use it. To ensure this does not happen, I have all my auto-ship items scheduled to ship on the 25th of the month. On the 15th of the month, I have a reminder in my calendar (on repeat) to check auto-ship. I check all my subscriptions and delay the ones I don't need next month. It keeps me from forgetting to order and ending up with more than I need.

Many things I've mentioned here are expensive, but they all last a long time. I didn't buy them all at once. Some were gifts, some I purchased refurbished, some I found on Facebook Marketplace. Pick the one issue that is most annoying to you today, and shop around. Then, in a few months, decide on the next thing you can improve, do your research, and shop around for the best solution.

For easy access to these recommendations, I added these to **EfficinecyBitch.com/FavoriteThings**.

DECLUTTER

If your house or office space is disorganized, so is your life. Keeping clutter picked up, trash removed, and basic cleaning done is simple if maintained every day, but it's easier said than done. Here are some of my favorite ways to keep my house organized.

The best way to eat an elephant is one bite at a time. Same thing with decluttering your home. Go through your home one room at a time to purge items you no longer need and plan to do it frequently. Each month schedule one room, area or closet to tackle. Add the name of the area as an "event" in your calendar on the first day of the month this year and as an annual repeat entry. Because items accumulate, you can't assume to declutter and that it will stay that way. You must plan to manage and maintain this process forever. But having a plan is half the battle.

My home is planned like this:

January – Holiday decoration storage

February – Junk Drawers / Closets

March – Garage

April – Office

May – Kids Playroom

June – Laundry Room

July – Garage

August – Master closet

September – Kids Playroom

October – Linen Closet

November – Kitchen

December – Kids clothes

You can choose to tackle the room the way that works best for you. Some projects can be done in a few hours. Other require a few days. You'll notice a few rooms happen more than once a year because they get messier and more cluttered faster. The trick is to plan your attack plan. Then one by one, go through each closet, drawer, and cabinet in the assigned room or area. Be prepared for trash, donation, and sale items. Come prepared with a vacuum, duster, and cleaning tools. If it's an area you do once a year, it will have accumulated a year worth of dust too.

This is time-consuming and can wear some people out. If it's not your thing, get help. Ask your partner, parents, kids, or friends to help you. You can even outsource this. I'm fortunate to have given presentations on small business accounting to a few chapters of the National Association of Professional Organizers. If you want help and need to find someone near you, look them up. A fantastic resource, and even more amazing woman, is Laurie Palau who hosts *This Organized Life* YouTube channel and podcast, which I have been honored to speak on. Laurie is also the author of *Hot Mess, A Practical Guide to Getting Organized*.[16] She has fantastic tips for getting through the clutter of your life more simply. Create easy systems to support your life without spending a fortune.

Bins help organize closets and drawers. If you do one cabinet or drawer a day, you will find the home is finished quickly. I like to buy drawer organizers at the dollar store or on sale. One of my favorite tricks is to use turntables inside cabinets. I learned this trick from a professional organizer in my town, Beverly. Beverly is the owner of Life Simply Organized, and the many great organization and functional tips she has on her Instagram page will blow your mind. Another little tip she taught me is to use labels on boxes that are in storage. For example, don't just label a box "Christmas Decorations." Instead, include its contents. This saves a lot of time both when you are looking for something and when you put items away after the holiday season. Everything fits right the first time when you know where it goes. So simple, right? So easy and doable that it'll make you wonder how you lived without it before.

I'm learning to be more conscious of the sustainability of what I buy and how I use it. I'm not buying as much, and if I do, I try to get it secondhand. The same goes with how I get rid of things. As I move through the house and find items I no longer need, I create listings on Facebook Marketplace. When these items belong to my kids I include them in the process, which helps them learn more about money. If after a few days, the items are not sold, I lower the price, or we take them to Goodwill. I repeat these steps throughout my house.

I'm also very deliberate with where things are stored. For example, I often go to the gym while the rest of my house sleeps. I get dressed in the dark. Since we have motion-sensor lights in my closet, it wakes my husband up if I go in there. Instead, I keep my workout clothes in the linen closet, all lined up together. I bought small bins for pants, sports bras, socks, and tank tops. My tennis shoes live in there, along with hair ties. Everything I need is in an easy-to-reach place, ready to grab even on the days I try to talk myself out of it. I have a similar system with the kids' lunches. We have an entire cabinet (lower cabinet, so they can reach it) in the kitchen for the kids to put their lunchboxes and water bottles. All the kid food is low in the refrigerator and pantry. The kids can easily access everything they need to fill and empty their lunchboxes daily.

TRAVEL SMARTER

As a "road warrior," a person who travels frequently for work, I have developed some specific routines and techniques that make traveling a million times easier. Travel stresses most people. You can tell that's true because the people who work in airports often look whiplashed from all the grumpy passengers that they manage day in and day out. Working in the travel industry isn't easy. As a hotel and restaurant management major in college, I knew travel would be part of my life. I just didn't know it would be such a large part. To keep travel as stress free as possible, follow these tips:

- Sign up for TSA PreCheck. It's valid for many years and speeds things up in security. It's worth its weight in gold.
- Fly the same airline when possible. Not only will you rack up miles, but you have the option to gain high reward status through loyalty programs. Road Warriors covet status. The benefits vary by airline, but many include free and priority bags, priority boarding, free snacks, airport lounge access, upgrades to First Class when available, and priority assistance for canceled and late flights.
- Use packing cubes. These handy cubes are my favorite to use when traveling to multiple destinations or with my family. Packing cubes allow me to bundle items in my suitcase for a specific day or task. For example,

I put all bathing suits for the whole family in one packing cube. Or I might put clothes for the second leg of the trip in a separate cube. Not only does it keep me organized, but it also helps compress the items, reducing wrinkles (crazy but true) and lets me fit more in the suitcase. Several sizes, colors, and designs are available at retailers like Bed Bath and Beyond, Target, and Amazon.

- Try to make all the outfits you pack work with one pair of shoes. I can hear the gasps from far and wide for all the shoe lovers out there, but bringing fewer shoes saves a lot of space. I will do anything not to have to check a bag (even when I do have status) since I've had my fair share of lost bags over the years.

- If you're a frequent traveler, consider keeping two sets of toiletries. I have a second set of makeup, hairbrush, deodorant, and more that I only use on trips. This helps save in packing and unpacking in both directions and makes life a lot easier. It also can be a life saver if your bag gets lost on its way home.

- Carry a spare identification card. I usually put mine in my toiletry bag in my suitcase. I also have a photograph of my passport on my phone in case the worst happens, and I lose my IDs. Airlines understand when this happens and have processes for helping you recover and get home but having these backups sure helps.

- Always pack the following in your carry-on: a reusable water bottle, book, notepad, and portable battery pack for your cellphone. As a nursing mom, I also carried a manual breast pump, saving me from extreme pain during unexpected delays on more than one occasion.

Managing the inboxes of your life is a never-ending task, but it can be simple if you are intentional with your actions. By simplifying your inboxes, you will increase your mental clarity, find more time to spend doing the things you love, and waste less time and money. Speaking of time, life's great equalizer, in the next chapter we will cover how to manage your time using three simple rules: delegate, automate, and eliminate.

*"Make a decision and stick to it. Professionally, this mantra saves
my mind from anxiously spinning and keeps me moving forward.
Physically, it conserves my energy and makes me resilient.
Emotionally, it keeps me present and content. Whether I'm signing
a new contract, declining a social event, signing up for a yoga class,
or planning time off for a family vacation, my actions are intentional.
So don't complicate it; decide and stick to it."*

Liann Delaney, mother of two
Co-Owner, Two Sense Consulting

CHAPTER 4

T for TIME

Time is the great equalizer, according to the Rule of 168. The Rule of 168 is simple math: seven days a week times twenty-four hours in a day. Bill Carmody says, "It doesn't matter how rich or successful you are—everyone gets only 168 hours each week. Period. You can't buy more time, but you can sell your available hours to someone else. This is what the wealthy refer to as leverage."[17]

Given that you cannot buy more time, and you never know when you will run out of it, time is arguably the most valuable resource a person has. The way you spend your time says a lot about you. It says what you prioritize, what you find value in, and what you want tomorrow to look like. Knowing how to leverage time is why some people can run ten businesses, while training for a marathon and becoming an award-winning author, while others stress out about their job and everyday life tasks.

The crazy thing about time is that just like money, it can shrink and expand depending on how we use it. An adage called Parkinson's Law says, "Work expands to fill the time available for its completion."[18] Simply stated, if you give someone one hour or three hours to complete the same task, they will likely use all the time allotted. You can modify and expand time if you are thoughtful and intentional with how you use it. Armed with this information, you can decide what to put your time into rather than what to fill your time with.

I am a working mom. That is my identity. I never entertained the idea of not being one, but when I became a mother, my daughter filled all my extra time, love, and thoughts. She made me work faster and harder so that I could go home to her sooner. My motivation had never been higher. When I had my second daughter, I got worried. For the first time, I questioned my ability to be a great mom and keep kicking ass at my career. I took a low profile role while I adjusted to life of being a mom of two and then two years later, pressed the accelerator again.

In 2014, one of my favorite mentors suggested I apply for a new role at my company's corporate office. My responsibilities included designing, implementing, and stabilizing massive change in my organization to centralize accounting. This role meant lots of exposure to many brilliant people and lots of domestic and international travel. I would be driving change for an entire division within the organization. Since the corporate headquarters were in Canada, I lived in Arizona, and the hotels were all over the world, it made more sense for me to work remotely (aka from home).

Pre-COVID-19 pandemic, working from home was very rare. In fact, my offer letter specifically stated that I must have an office dedicated to working and not let other stakeholders realize that I was a remote employee. Despite some reservations about the frequent travel, I took the role and fell in love with the work. I thrived in this challenging, exciting role. The company encouraged and rewarded me for using my instincts to move this change forward. Everything was going great—at work and at home. I had happy daughters and a career waiting to be explored. Then it happened. I was pregnant again.

Suddenly, I found myself in a tricky spot. My wish of being a mom again came true, but at a pivotal time in my career. I had just taken a role that had the potential to take me to new professional levels and success. How would I fulfill the expectations of the job and care for my infant and two toddlers? I knew significant life decisions were ahead. I set my mind to making it work. I had the good fortune of working in an incredibly forward-thinking organization that had always been great to its employees; I could make this happen.

I will never forget telling my boss as we drove to dinner when I was visiting the office one week. I hadn't even had an ultrasound yet, but I knew he needed to know as soon as possible. I felt terrified. I assured him that I would not let him down, and I didn't.

Those first few years were very hard. I flew 100,000-150,000 miles annually across multiple continents. Not only did I fight constant jetlag, but also the physical strain of breastfeeding. On more than one occasion I had to pump on an airport bathroom floor. When I worked from home, I balanced all of it: laundry, school pickups, PTO meetings, conference calls, and so much more. When not at home, I worried constantly that I'd forgotten to leave information for my husband or mother-in-law.

My mother-in-law retired a few years before I took on my new role, and she volunteered to help us during this crazy new time. She frequently made the two-hour drive from her home to ours to help my husband while I traveled. I traveled every other week, which added a lot of pressure on Steve while he managed his own career. Asking for and accepting help is not always easy, but when the opportunity presents itself, take it. Having help made me feel less guilty for leaving and kept Steve from coming to resent my career. And it most definitely kept the kids happy.

I almost had a nervous breakdown more than once. I was depressed, stressed, overweight and frustrated. I was at rock bottom, but no one knew. Instead, they all saw the confident exterior I projected. As difficult as those years were, they were critical to my development into becoming who I am today. I don't regret a single moment of the strain, but I wish I had known then what I know now about managing time.

I pushed myself hard—probably harder than I should have. But I wanted to prove that I could be a role model to my kids. I wanted them to see a mom who followed her dreams and loved them fiercely. To do and be both, I had to learn time management. During these years, I discovered the secrets to my success: delegate, automate, and eliminate.

DELEGATE

I didn't figure it out all at once. I took it one step at a time and improved each day. But I needed something to work toward and didn't know how to take the first step. Then one day I listened to Rachel Hollis speak on her podcast about her *Start Today Journal*.[19] In this journal, she encourages the development of a big dream to design your goals. I bought her journal and started the process.

I laid out what I wanted my life to be like—the biggest dream I could imagine. With no limits in mind, I wrote: "I want a 3,000-square-foot, one-story home with a pool, in-ground trampoline, and home gym. I want to own my own business, become an author, and contribute to my community. I want to stay married to my best friend, remain connected to him, and live long, healthy lives together. I want to raise children who are well-rounded, love each other, and themselves. I want to learn to play golf, to camp with my family once a month, and to exercise five days a week. I want to be free of numbing agents like alcohol and make healthy choices for my body. I want to read ten pages a day of non-fiction and wake up at 5:00 a.m. every day." It was a tall order, but I was determined to get it.

From that day forward, I fell in love with my future self. I went out of my way to set myself up for success. When I wrote all these things down, it seemed like a long shot. Never in my wildest dreams did I think it could all actually happen. Spoiler alert, I'm living the reality of every one of those dreams today.

I realized quickly that the number of tasks I had on my plate left absolutely no room to add anything else to help me achieve my dreams. So, I started a new plan. Delegate! I needed to make more time in my day to be able to work on the goals I set for myself. I started with a list. I sat down and wrote down every little thing that I manage, inventory, or think about for the house and kids:

- Get the mail
- Pay the bills
- Take kids to school / daycare
- Pick the kids up from school / daycare
- Get school supplies
- Supervise homework / projects
- Bathe the kids
- Pack school lunches
- Prepare dinner
- Plan our kids' birthdays

- Coordinate for our kids to attend other kids' birthday parties
- Schedule and attend holiday events
- Go grocery shopping
- Scoop dog poop
- Feed the dog
- Bathe the dog
- Buy teacher gifts
- Handle car maintenance
- Put gas in the car
- Do the laundry
- Do the dishes
- Pick up toys
- Manage afterschool activities
- Coordinate home and car service appointments
- Clean the house
- Mow the lawn
- Coordinate Doctor appointments
- Wash the sheets
- Wash the towels

Once I had an exhaustive list, I showed my husband. To my surprise, he added a few things to the list. From there we divided the tasks as evenly as we could. Since that day, we have these tasks split up in mostly the same way. He takes half; I take half. He takes the kids to school; I pick them up. He makes dinner; I make breakfast.

I'm not going to lie. Starting didn't come easy. Tasks he did felt like "wife tasks," so I felt guilty as hell for having him "help me." I had to bite my tongue not to call out my morning checklist as he took the kids to school. But I had to let him and the kids find their own routine. Eventually, Steve and the kids created their own checklists and became surprisingly more capable than I gave any of them credit for. Things didn't always get done exactly the way I wanted at first, but that only lasted a few days. I can't say I loved the feeling of not being in control, but I did love the extra hours I had in the day to put toward my big goals. Soon enough, we adapted to a new routine, and we were all better for it.

I also experienced a brief period when I felt like less of a mom to my kids. I loved them as much as I always did, but I felt less needed, and, quite frankly, less overworked than I once had. It took some tough internal conversations with myself and external conversations with my husband to finally feel comfortable living this new life.

If you already have children, consider delegating tasks to them as well. Before you and your partner divide the tasks, see what you can give to your kids. Children need to be contributors to the household. My kids are responsible for cleaning their bedrooms, putting away some laundry, washing the sliding glass door, emptying and loading the dishwasher, and picking up dog waste. My kids are young, so they can't do all of it all the time, but I can start the habit now so that they contribute. They each have responsibilities, and they also have ticket-earning tasks. Tickets can be exchanged for screentime or money to buy candy or a treat from the ice cream truck. They love being helpful, and they are learning money and time management.

If you are single or don't have kids, consider other ways you can delegate tasks. Are there people in your neighborhood you can trade tasks with or pay to help you? In my experience there are often people near you who are willing and able to help, all you have to do is ask. If you don't know people in your area, consider apps like Task Rabbit or Fiver to find people who are offering services for reasonable prices.

While we are on the topic of getting help, one sure fire way to up level up your delegation: outsource it. I outsource everything I possibly can. The more I outsource, the more time I recover to make new money and the faster the return on investment. Some people flinch when I suggest this concept. Our culture has programed women to believe we must do it all. We don't. Outsourcing is not for the rich. Outsourcing is how ambitious people maintain order, build wealth, and gain time pursuing happiness.

As of 2022, an average family in the United States has 1.93 children.[20] If both parents work outside the home, that's a combined total of eighty working hours. The average commute in the U.S. is twenty-seven minutes, or four-and-a-half hours of commuting per week per person.[21] When they get home, there's homework to review, dishes to clean, kids to bathe, dogs to walk, bills to pay, and food to cook. This does not include laundry, landscaping, cleaning toilets, vacuuming, mopping floors, or running errands. Playtime with the kids happens for a few minutes each day, leaving parents longing for a closer connection with their children and each other. This scenario is far too common. It creates more fatigue, frustration, and parental guilt—and most of it hits women right between the eyes. After all, who's ever heard of "dad guilt."

The solution is simple: outsource the things you don't like. If you don't like doing laundry, send it to a laundry service. If you don't like cleaning, pay someone to come a few times a month. If you don't like yard work, hire a landscaper. Many people view these services as luxuries, but it's the opposite. Outsourcing is for busy people who have their eyes on a better life and want to reap the benefits of their hard work. Outsourcing costs money, so start slowly. Rearranging your budget and eliminating items of lesser importance can help you find more time in your life for play. I suggest finding the thing you hate the most and building a path to outsource that one thing. I started with housecleaning.

My childhood memory of housecleaning is doing it as a family on the weekends. The house seemed free of clutter all the time, but the deep cleaning had to be done after the soccer games on Saturday. That was the case until my mom was diagnosed with breast cancer my freshman year of high school, which led to the first time my family hired help. Her name was Nora. My mom says, "Your dad hired a housekeeper for me when I got cancer." I remember that phrase catching my attention back then, and I have the same reaction today when she says it. *He* hired Nora to take the pressure off *mom*. He knew she would feel the obligation, responsibility, and requirement to clean, so he created conditions to relieve her of them.

Nora quickly became part of our family. My mother always gave her birthday gifts, holiday gifts, and "just because" gifts. Nora did the same for us. My mom spent time talking to her, hearing about her kids, and telling her about us. They were friends. More than that, Nora became an extension of the role my mom felt she had to play in the home. If my mom had not gotten cancer, I wonder if she would have ever accepted the help. But, once mom had Nora, she never let her go.

Nora stayed with my family for twenty-five years. She came every week when we were young, every two weeks as we got older, and once a month long after we had moved out. She attended our graduation parties, weddings, and baby showers. She will always be a special part of my family.

When I first moved away from home, I did not have a housekeeper. When Steve and I started a family, we didn't have a housekeeper either. I did it. Then, around the fifth month of my pregnancy with our second child, my mom suggested we hire someone to help with the cleaning. I hesitated. I felt guilty. I didn't need help. I only had one kid, and I was healthy (in my mind I correlated hiring help with my mom's cancer). I could figure it out. When I protested, my mom insisted. She compromised that she would pay for monthly cleaning services for me until the baby came. After that, Steve and I needed to find a way to afford it. She knew the benefits of getting help and would not let me wait as long as she had. I agreed.

I asked a few people at work and found a few leads. We interviewed three women by phone. I invited two of them to see the house and provide an estimate. Their estimates were based on several factors, including the size of the home, overall cleanliness, number of bedrooms, and the number of times they would come a month. The more often they visited, the less it cost each time because the house stayed cleaner.

We started off with monthly visits, which cost $200. Then, we switched to every two weeks, which cost $150 each visit. Now, with three kids and a dog, we need weekly visits for $100. Our cost has gone up, but so has the cleanliness of our home. The amazing women who clean for us have become my friends. I care about them and the wellbeing of their families. They are an extension of my team, not my "hired help." We exchange holiday gifts and ask about each other's kids.

Like my mom before me, once I started, I never went back. The gift of cleaning once a month made me realize how much time I was spending cleaning bathrooms when I could have been playing with my baby. Steve and I consider this a non-negotiable household expense. We would sooner get rid of the cable bill than our housecleaning team. Whenever people ask me for tips on being more efficient, having a housecleaning service is the first thing I suggest. The return on investment is quick. I don't have to buy expensive cleaning solutions, fancy vacuums, or mops. My team brings their own equipment and supplies and can clean the house in an eighth of the time it takes me.

Even if you feel you can't afford a housekeeping service, I encourage you to get a quote. It's easy to say, "I can't afford it." What you really might mean is, "I don't want help doing what I think is my role as a wife and/or mother." Test yourself. Get the quote and then decide if you can't afford it. You may need to shave a little money off your "Might Buy" list to afford it. But consider how much time and energy you will save, not to mention the offset in cleaning supplies. Furthermore, not only will you be helping yourself, but you are also supporting someone else's business. I have encountered people who say they feel guilty for having someone else clean their homes. It triggers a sense of privilege or laziness or "wife guilt" for not doing what their mothers did. Based on what we know about the expectations of the women who came before us, it's realistic to expect women today to experience this type of guilt. But if someone provides a service as a housecleaner, you should not feel any different than if they were cleaning your hotel room, fixing your car, or bagging your groceries. They are offering you a service, and you are paying for it. This is not free labor, and you are not taking advantage of anyone. You can negotiate a fair price, and so can they.

There are different types of cleaners available to hire. You can go to a corporation that does background checks and pays their cleaners by the hour. You can find housekeepers who are paid independently. They are professionals who perform specific tasks at a particular time for a fair price. You should establish a day of the week and time when they arrive and hold yourself to it. For example, the house needs to be tidied before they come. Removing clutter before they clean will ensure they can do their job to the fullest and that you get the most from it. Letting go and delegating tasks like this will free up hours for you to do the things you love.

"Just like you're not going to love every aspect of your career,
you won't love everything about motherhood—and that's okay.
I'm not a huge fan of accounting and I outsource that to professionals
to handle. As for motherhood, you may need to do the same thing."

Jayd Hernandez, mother of two
Owner and Camouflage Tattoo Artist, Studio Conceal

AUTOMATE

What I can't delegate, I automate. Some things I automate with technology, which you learned about in the previous chapter. Other things I automate with my behavior using routines. In his book *The Power of Habit*, Charles Duhigg talks about the habit loop required to turn a new behavior into a habit: cue, routine, reward.[22] The best of any new habit I've implemented in my life is the habit of becoming a morning person.

I have a truth bomb to lay down, and you may not like it: efficiency is born in the morning. Many people declare themselves night owls and fight against getting up early. I get it; I used to be one of them. When our oldest turned one, we put her on a strict sleep schedule. I felt passionate that setting up a solid sleep routine for our kids would be a priority when they were young. I didn't realize while doing this that if I taught our kids to be good sleepers and morning people, I would have to be one too. Since they were babies, my kids have always had an early bedtime. Asleep by eight and most of the time, they wake up at five or six in the morning. This training is great when you have to get up to go to work or school, but it's not so fun on the weekends, especially if you let your inner night owl soar until 2:00 a.m.

Once I realized how much time I spent fighting against being a morning person, I decided to make a change. I forced myself, kicking and screaming, to become a morning person. One of the best tools I used to develop this new way of life is *The Miracle Morning* by Hal Elrod.[23] Elrod developed a system (and acronym) for creating a morning routine that will change your life. And you know what? It works!

His acronym is S.A.V.E.R.S. It stands for Silence, Affirmations, Visualization, Exercise, Read, Scribing. He digs deep into the reasons and ways to set your morning up for this new routine, and I can vouch for its effectiveness. I began working on my "power hour," and within three weeks, my life had been transformed.

Today, I am an avid believer in the benefits of being a morning person. Waking up early and being in control of the first hour of your day in a way that fills your mind and spirit is so energizing. The trick is understanding that your morning start time does not have to be at 5:00 a.m. It can start when you want it to, but it does mean waking up at least an hour before anyone or anything else needs your attention. For example, get up at seven o'clock if you have to start getting ready for work at eight o'clock. If you have to be up with your kids at six o'clock, wake up a five o'clock. If you have to start school at eleven o'clock, start your morning at ten o'clock. Give yourself an hour to gain your power before doing anything else. My kids leave the house for school at 7:15 a.m. This means they are out of bed around 6:30 a.m. This also means that I'm needed at 6:30 a.m. Therefore, I wake up between 5:00 a.m. and 5:30 a.m. every day, even on weekends.

Here's how my day starts:

My Apple Watch wakes me up using an app called Auto Sleep. It detects when I'm in my lightest sleep between 5:00 a.m. and 5:30 a.m. so that I wake feeling rested. I turn on the Keurig coffeemaker and start my cup of coffee. While it's brewing, I slip into my office to get my book, phone, pen, and EB Daily Action Plan.

I'll pause here to tell you a little about my EB Daily Action Plan. I'm not a "day planner" kind of girl. I use Google Calendar to track all my appointments and meetings. Using a day planner always felt unnatural to me. However, I do like to set up an action plan for my day with paper and pen. Something about writing it out helps prepare me for the day ahead. I couldn't find a tool that worked for me, so I made my own version. With some help from my amazing friend and admin, Janelle, we made it pretty and ready for you to download.

The EB Daily Action Plan has five sections on the first page: on my mind, goals, appointments, to-do, and upcoming events. I'll explain these below. The second page is for nighttime use. It is every bit as important to me as the morning page, so that I can go to sleep knowing I'm ready for what's coming. Download a copy at **EfficiencyBitch.com/ActionPlan**.

Okay, so I've grabbed everything I need from my office. I drop it all next to the coffeemaker. I move onto the rug in the center of my living room to stretch for a few minutes. Nothing super fancy, just enough to get my joints loosened up and my neck and back woken up. (I suffer from neck tension from sitting at a desk most of my life, so this little morning stretch helps a lot.) I drink my coffee black, so by the time I'm done stretching, it's had a few minutes to cool off. I grab it and make my way to my comfy chair or, depending on the time of year, out to the backyard to enjoy the morning weather. I spend the first few minutes sitting in silence. I let my mind wander, and thoughts enter and exit my mind. Maybe it could be considered meditation, but not formally. I just sit. Nothing else. After about two minutes, I write a few words on my EB Daily Action Plan, whatever is on my mind. Maybe it's something I'm worried about, or excited about. Maybe it's the song lyrics of the cartoon my kids watch on repeat. I write whatever is in my head.

Next, I move to the goals section. I write three goals: one short-term (today), one near-term (this month), and one long-term (year). I write them all in the past tense as if I have already accomplished them. Today my goals are:

- **Today:** I walked 10,000 steps.
- **This month:** I added the school holidays and half-days to my calendar for the year.
- **This year:** I became a published author.

These are not "saving the world" type goals. They are things I want to do, I plan to do, and I commit to do. Writing them down helps me stay committed.

Next, I look at my phone to see if any personal or family appointments are going to interrupt my workday. Things like doctor appointments, piano lessons, or a veterinarian appointment for the dog. This is everything that must get done around my work schedule. I don't add work meetings or tasks to this list because, by and large, work comes easier to me than household stuff. Although I don't want this to become a full day planner, if there's something different than the usual workflow, I may add it to my EB Daily Action Plan—like speaking to a women's group, for example.

Then, I look ahead in the week. Is there anything I need to prepare for? This may be work or personal, like having a presentation on Friday or needing to bring snacks to the Saturday basketball game. Anything I need to keep in the back of mind for the next few days gets written down.

The last section is my to-do list. This is usually long and carries over day after day. I look at my to-do list from yesterday and move over any items that I didn't complete. I know it seems redundant to rewrite it all, but in doing so I gain a new perspective on it. By rewriting it, I check if I can eliminate, automate or delegate anything. Sometimes this is part of the "invisible load," but other times it's a specific task that I don't want to forget:

- Art supplies for school tomorrow
- Get oil change in car
- Snacks for baseball tomorrow
- The trash needs to be put on the curb
- Two of the three kids need a lunch packed today; the third gets hot lunch
- Unpack fall sweatshirts

By this time, it's nearing 5:20 a.m. I head into my bedroom to change into my workout clothes and tennis shoes. I fill up my gallon water bottle, then spend the next ten to fifteen minutes (whatever is left until 5:50 a.m.) reading TheSkimm, an e-newsletter that I subscribe to.[24] It offers cliff notes of yesterday's news. If there are things I'm interested in, the link to the full article is there to dig deeper. It's a fast way to get yesterday's headlines without getting caught up in opinion pieces or clickbait. If I finish early, I always have a book ready. I love self-help and business development books. They get my brain thinking and considering new points of view first thing in the morning.

At 5:50 a.m. on the dot, I walk out the door to the gym. Finding a gym that I like has taken a long time. I've tried them all. The best gym is the one you will go to with consistency. Mine is three minutes from my house. The workout is group weightlifting circuit training for forty-five minutes and they charge me if I sign up but don't show up. I love the added motivation it gives me because I hate wasting money. Only choose this type of gym if you also are motivated by not wasting money. Otherwise, it's money down the drain. If you *do* have a habit of throwing money down the drain, don't commit to a gym like this until you've kicked that habit.

Some days, I chose not to schedule time at the gym. Instead, I do yoga at home or walk my dog. Other days, I ride my bike or go for a jog. It's not always the gym, but it's always a move-my-body activity at 5:50 a.m. that lasts thirty to forty-five minutes.

To ensure my family doesn't have to rely on me to wake them, I set up Amazon Alexa to complete "routines" at the same time every day. One of these routines occurs at 6:30 a.m. every morning. The routine plays music throughout the house to slowly wake everyone up. Finally, at 6:45 a.m., the alarm starts. As the kids get up, they go into the kitchen to start breakfast. I have a dedicated bin in the pantry with the items needed for the kids' usual breakfast requests. Our kids love frozen blueberry waffles with peanut butter and jelly, and a side of chocolate milk. This has been their staple breakfast for as long as I can remember. Occasionally, my son asks for cinnamon toast, so the bin contains Ovaltine chocolate milk powder, peanut butter, cinnamon sugar, bread, and their multivitamins. Until recently, our kids needed help making breakfast, but in the last year or so, everyone has learned to make their own. The bin helps them get everything out at once and makes clean-up easy.

Our kids make their own lunches as part of their afterschool routine, so all we have to do in the morning is add ice packs and fill water bottles. After the kids are dressed and fed, they are free to play or watch television until Alexa announces, "It's 7:05. Five minutes until we leave for school." The kids know this is their cue to brush their teeth, put on their shoes, and grab their lunch. Five minutes later, Alexa announces, "It's 7:10. Time for school. Have a great day!"

Let me pause here to say my children are not perfect. They don't follow these commands like little robots. The prompts set up habits for them to become more self-sufficient. Steve and I still do a lot of reminding. The value of this automated routine with Alexa is that we are not the time-keepers. It's also teaching our kids to use alarms to help them develop into punctual adults.

Steve drives the kids to school, so I use this time to get ready. I am showered and dressed for the day by 7:30 a.m. I give myself twenty minutes in the morning to get showered and ready. I used to waste over an hour getting ready in the morning until I realized Parkinson's Law applied: I was giving myself too much time to complete something that didn't need it. I go from the shower to my shoes in twenty minutes. Some people think that's crazy, but I'm telling you it can be done. All it takes is a little intention. One trick I learned recently is to create (or hire help creating) a capsule wardrobe that can be diverse and mix and matched to your style quickly. I have about twenty pieces of clothing in my closet, but the combinations are endless. I find having fewer options makes getting ready easier. To find help in this space I would recommend searching Collective Wardrobes or Capsule Wardrobes and see who pops up in your area.

Next, I head to the kitchen to make myself a morning protein shake with greens and multivitamins. Finally, I can start my workday feeling organized, energized, focused, and ready to kick ass and take names.

I am pretty dang consistent with this routine. Of course, I'm far from perfect; some days I don't get out of bed on time, a kid wakes up late, or I have a meeting with someone on the east coast who forgets that 9:00 a.m. Eastern Time is 6:00 a.m. Pacific Time. Still, I strive to practice this routine four to five days a week. I also modify my routine a little based on the weather. I live in Arizona, so the winters are glorious, but it's dark until 7:00 a.m., and I won't walk the streets alone in the dark. The hot summers are miserable; it's ninety degrees by 6:00 a.m. The point is not to be rigid, but to be intentional about a process that works to cluster your morning with the things your mind, body, and spirit need most.

This routine may seem overwhelming, but I promise you it works. You do it a few times, feel the reward, and create a habit. The first few mornings will be challenging, but you will find your energy, break through the inertia, and set yourself up to feel great. By 8:00 a.m., you'll look at your day and know precisely what you have to get done to succeed. Getting your circadian rhythm synced to your new early-bird routine may take a few days, but it will catch up. Soon, by 9:00 p.m., you will be ready for bed if for no other reason than the reward of the great next morning.

I believe a good evening routine can help set up your mornings for the best success. In my pre-mom days, I loved evenings. It meant binge-watching my favorite Netflix series, happy hour with friends, or finishing schoolwork while completing my master's degree. Today, evenings are the most challenging time of day for me. I want to be the best version of myself for my family, but it's very taxing. I look for ways to improve my evening routine to end my day with as much peace and intention as I start my day.

Have you ever heard of the Witching Hour?[25] The Witching Hour, when used in the context of children (not the supernatural), is a predictable and repeated time of day, typically in the late afternoon, evening, and into the early night hours (usually between the hours of 5:00 p.m. to 12:00 a.m.) when your otherwise happy baby is inconsolable. It's typically used in the context of infants, but I'm here to tell you school-aged children and adults can also experience it. I have fought the Witching Hour evening routine, anxiety, and expectations as long as I've been a mother. My evenings are still not the incredible bliss that my mornings are, but I do have tips that make it go a little more smoothly.

No two days look the same, so designing a perfect routine is impossible. Every day combines homework, doctor appointments, sports practice, after-school clubs or lessons, and that pesky thing we all think needs to be picture perfect…dinner! None of my kids play sports competitively yet, but they are into many different things. One has Girl Scouts, piano lessons, and volleyball. The second has baseball, karate, and basketball. The third has drama rehearsal and photography. They all have homework and tests to study for. Not only is it a lot to manage on the calendar, but it's also a lot of equipment to keep track of.

Cleats, gloves, balls, jerseys, scripts, music books, and cameras. To limit the time spent on a scavenger hunt, I designated the coat closet near the back door as the "sports closet." I purchased an inexpensive, hanging organizer to create cubbies and drawers, so I could keep all the items we need for these activities in this closet. When jerseys are washed, they are hung in the sports closet. When practice is over, all the items are placed back in the sports closet. If an item is found anywhere in the house outside the closet, which happens all the time, we ask that child to pick it up and put it back in its proper place. I keep the items not needed for the current season in the garage or on the top shelf of the sports closet. If they outgrow the item, I put it up for sale on Facebook Marketplace or drop it off at Goodwill. The items in the sports closet are current and organized.

Each night, we talk as a family about the events that are happening the next day. I remind my son that he has basketball after school and needs to wear tennis shoes to school. I remind my daughter that she has to charge her camera batteries the night before her photography club meets. This simple routine of looking at the calendar the night before and ensuring all the items we need are in their proper place takes five minutes and saves us about thirty minutes of stress the next day. We have a whiteboard in the kitchen where the kids write down any events that they have the following day as a reminder. As we call out our tasks for tomorrow, the kids write them down. The board serves a few purposes:

1. The kids learn to appreciate to-do lists and plan their day.
2. They see the list again the next morning, and when they get home from school.
3. They get additional writing and reading practice.
4. Hopefully, they grow up to be an EB too.

Depending on the day, we may go straight from school to a lesson or head home first. If I know we're going from school to practice, I load the items in the car the night before. I also pack a snack bag and water bottle. I learned it's better to be prepared on these days than hope that I will have time to remember on the day of the activity itself. On the days I don't prep ahead, I always seem to have a client call that runs late, so I have no time to grab a snack, and we end up at a gas station for a donut on the way to practice. I'm not anti-sugar for my kids, but I try to save money and extra calories as much as possible.

Another variable is how many kids will be with me at each practice. Part of the planning includes who will be telling me they are bored. I keep books, toys, or a ball they can play with in the car to stay entertained while waiting for their sibling. I don't feel obligated to watch every practice with my full attention. Sure, I want to see my kids learn and play, but watching them run the same drill over and over can be mind-numbing. I use this time to answer emails and pay bills online. These little pockets of time can be great for productivity if you plan for them and have little tasks assigned for them. I'm deliberate with what tasks I do in each section of idle time. This preparation allows me to focus on homework and dinner when we get home.

Dinner is a touchy subject for me. I don't particularly like food. I'll eat because I must, but it's not something I get excited about. As a child, I was an extremely picky eater, and while I've learned to manage it as an adult, I'd still rather eat the same three things every day. My daughter is this way too; she's pickier than I am and has been diagnosed with Avoidant/Restrictive Food Intake Disorder (ARFID). For her and for us, it's a frustrating anxiety disorder that stems from fear of food.

Needless to say, mealtime can be very tough in our house, mainly at dinnertime. I'm certain my lack of desire to think about, talk about, or cook food exaggerated her aversions. Still, there is nothing this child will eat. My other two kids and my husband all love food. Balancing the mixed bag of palates at our dinner table is complicated. Add to this the subconscious pressure of society telling me I needed to have dinner on the table every night, and you have yourself the proverbial pressure cooker. I've tried everything. Some things have worked, and others haven't. Meal planning has worked best for us. I keep it simple with three strategies:

1. **Staples:** Maintain a list of items you always need. Basics that every-one eats and likes or fast meals. Keep these items saved as favorites if you shop online with delivery.

2. **Shop your pantry:** Before you go to the store, inventory of the items you have in the house on Sundays. It's amazing how many items you forget you already have. First, go through the staples list and see what you need more of. Then consider three meals you can make with the items you already have. Add the missing items to your list. I recommend starting with three meals over seven days. This allows you to have leftovers two nights, a wildcard night, and the opportunity to eat out once a week if you like.

3. **Place the order.** Shop online and have your groceries delivered when possible. In most cases you can tell the store which items they can make substitutions for if your selection is unavailable, and which items they can't. Next choose a delivery time and place the order. This helps curb impulse purchases at the store and saves an enormous amount of time. Even after paying the driver's tip and delivery fee, my order costs $30.00 less on average than if I shop in the store. There may be items you want to pick out— produce and meat, for example. When this occurs, make a list and spend no more than ten minutes in the store when necessary.

The common response I hear to online shopping orders is that people enjoy browsing the grocery aisles. Retailers enjoy the fact that you do this too. If you enjoy shopping and browsing in person, allow yourself to do it once or twice a month. Use the other two or three weeks to spend that time on something more productive. You will become more efficient and spend less money.

Once you know what you want to make for dinner that week, look at the activities that will take over the evenings and plan your meals accordingly. Think ahead about what makes sense to eat each night of the week. Does it make sense to prepare a complicated dish the night you have two sport events? Maybe that night is better suited for a crockpot meal or leftovers.

Give yourself realistic time and energy when meal planning, or you'll end up frustrated and hungry in the drive thru.

I am not the chef in our house; Steve is. A lot of women hate to cook, but they do it because it's expected of them. Meanwhile, their husbands like to cook but have been encouraged to "stay out of the kitchen." As I shared earlier, many reasons exist to explain why men brought home the bacon, and women fried it. Those reasons might have made sense at the time; they may or may not still have value for you and your situation.

I encourage you to share cooking responsibilities with others in your home. If you like to cook, rock on. If you don't, talk to the people you live with and see if they would be into taking on parts of it. If neither of you likes to cook, or you are doing life solo, consider a meal box subscription to simplify the process. Once I stopped worrying about "my responsibility" that an invisible societal audience put on me, I gave myself permission not to worry about my role at dinnertime. I began to realize that it's not my duty in life to cook all the meals for my family every day. My job is to work with my partner to feed our children and teach them reasonable methods to feed themselves. It's a family responsibility, not just mom's.

Now, let's circle back to the second page of the EB Daily Action Plan. With my EB Daily Action Plan for Tonight in hand, I take all the above into consideration. Writing it all down gets it off my mind so I can sleep well. I write a few affirmations, as Hal Elrod suggests. This helps me implant messages into my subconscious about what I want to hold on to or become. A couple examples are, "I wake up at 5:00 a.m. every day." "I am strong in mind and body." An app I like is called Think Up, which allows you to re-cord your voice saying these affirmations and play them back to yourself. I have found this both easy and effective.

Next, I write down anything I need to prepare for tomorrow. This will be rewritten in the morning, but it gets it off my brain at bedtime. I write down any new to-do items that came my way during the day, so I can easily incorporate into tomorrow's list.

I added a section at the bottom of the sheet to reflect on items I pur-chased that day. I did this to help curb some of the impulse purchasing habit

I formed online shopping during the COVID-19 pandemic. I was overusing and overbuying items because it was simply so easy. I added this reflection to my routine so I could review the items I purchased and decide if I really needed them or not. It helped me quickly catch unhelpful spending patterns and raised my awareness of how I was spending money that could be saved instead.

The last part of the sheet is a simple checklist—because I love checking things off a list. Every day I am motivated to do these five little things simply because it's on a list and I want to check them off:

- ✓ Exercise
- ✓ Water
- ✓ Vitamins
- ✓ Read
- ✓ Stretch

After this little catch-up with myself, I'm ready for the next day and prepared to take on anything the day might bring.

ELIMINATE

When you can't delegate or automate, look for what you can eliminate. In some cases, it may be better to eliminate *before* you automate or delegate.

Spam

Some of the things you can eliminate are obvious, but annoying to manage—spam solicitation, for example. We all get spam. We all hate it. If the amount of spam you receive seems to have grown over the years, it's because it has. Bots are all over the Internet grabbing up your phone number and email address for advertising and marketing purposes. Try this: every time you get a spam phone call or text message, block their number from calling you again. It may seem like you're doing this daily for a while, but eventually it will slow down. Will it ever stop? Probably not. But the more unreachable your number is, the less valuable it will be to solicitation, and over time you'll get called less often.

Eliminate email spam. We talked about keeping your email inbox clean in the I for Inbox chapter but be sure to eliminate the extra noise here too.

When you open your email today, take a few moments to unsubscribe from all the emails you got today and wish you hadn't. Do the same tomorrow and the next day. Within ten days or so you will have knocked out about 75 percent of your spam emails. Don't get discouraged if they come back. This is a lather, rinse, repeat cycle. Every time you buy something, you're added to new email lists. Make "unsubscribe" part of your daily inbox review.

Interruptions

Eliminate pointless interruptions. Go into your smartphone notifications and turn off everything that isn't mission critical. Limit notifications to meeting reminders (fifteen minutes before), text messages, phone calls, and alerts from critical apps. All other possible notifications are turned off. When you need a notification for an activity that isn't part of your daily routines, turn it on temporarily. For example, if you are traveling and want the airline to ping you about flight changes, enable notifications from the airline. If your kids play on a basketball team and the coach uses apps to communicate, allow those during the basketball season. Everything else is eliminated. They are distractions. Check your phone settings to see how often you're distracted by notifications. You should be able to find which apps send you messages, interrupting your day, and the amount of time you spend on them. In your phone settings, you can also set limits on your apps and screentime. This may take fifteen or twenty minutes, but it will save you time in the long run and provide fewer interruptions every day from now on. Remember that many apps automatically install with notifications automatically turned on. You may need to check this occasionally to keep it clean.

Track Your Time

One of the best tools to determine what tasks can be eliminated is to pay close attention to how you spend your time. For example, I track how the kids use technology with software like Circle Home, Bark, or Qustudio. I track how I spend time at work, documenting my admin, marketing, and client time. I track how much I sleep, exercise, and scroll on social media. These very easy-to-use apps come standard on smartphones. Look for the Health, Fitness, and Screen Time apps. Once you have data on how much time you really spend on activities (instead of how much time you *think* you spend), you can make changes accordingly.

Simplify

Another way to eliminate work is to review complex processes and systems. One of the best ways to remove "background noise" is to simplify it. This goes for a closet as well as the work you do. Consider tasks that are very complicated and work to simplify them. If the job needs to stay as complex as it is, it may be an excellent opportunity to outsource it. Letting an expert take on overly complicated tasks can save you time and energy. One example (and a chance for a shameless plug for Two Sense Consulting) is outsourcing your small business's bookkeeping. It's complex by nature. Handing it over to a professional allows them to review and simplify the process, even if only to hand it back to you. Never underestimate the power of a third opinion.

Finally, a note to elevate idle time that could be used productively. I'm not suggesting multi-tasking, as multi-tasking can result in less productive time and is generally proven to be more harmful than helpful. Instead, pair tasks that require no thought. It's called Habit Stacking. The idea is that you pair a new habit you want to something you already do all the time. For example, when you brush your teeth (old habit), do squats or leg lifts (new habit). Pretty soon the two go hand in hand. Consider how easily bad habits "stack themselves." Ever heard someone say, "I only smoke when I drink" or "I eat a bag of chips while watching television." Same idea. Think of one thing you do on autopilot and add something else simple to it. You'll be surprised by how easy it is to do.

Batching tasks is another great way to eliminate rework or "do it again" work. I love to batch folding socks. I have a basket in the laundry room that all clean, unpaired socks go into. Once a week I bring it into the living room, and we roll them as a family. If anyone needs clean socks before this day, they can go get them and find a pair themselves. Another very common batching habit is meal prepping or paying bills. Take out the trash in the entire house rather than one can at a time. Wash everyone's sheets on the same day rather than one at a time. I do fitted sheets first with pillowcases. Top sheets and comforters next. Then I can make parts of the bed for the whole house at once and batch parts to make it go a little smother.

To start, take your list of tasks from your inbox and identify which ones you can eliminate. Then go back to what you can delegate and automate. For good measure, do one more round of elimination; sometimes you'll see it differently on the second pass. When you've completed your list, take on the easy items first. This will help you gain momentum and confidence. Once you've established a rhythm and feel good, start to take on a more complicated item. You will amaze yourself at how fast this process will be and how much your future self will thank you.

> " *Work hard, mom hard, and take time for yourself.*
> *Be where your feet are. When you're at work, stay focused on*
> *the task. When you're at home, stay focused on your family.*
> *When it's time for you, stay focused on you.* "

Emily Hooten, mother of three
Area Director, Therapy and Beyond, BCBA

CHAPTER 5

C for CONNECTION

I am what you would call a social butterfly, but in small groups. I don't love big parties, but I really love people. I genuinely find people interesting and like to learn from them and their stories. I gain energy from people. But not everyone is extroverted like me. Introverts recharge their energy by being alone. No matter how you are naturally wired, this chapter will discuss how to connect with people when you are with them. Being part of the right groups of people and the strength of your relationships is a big part of the secret sauce to being an Efficiency Bitch.

YOU ARE WHAT YOU EAT

Consider this adage: you are what you eat. Now expand it to include everything you *consume*. You are what you consume, and we consume media and advertising messages more than any other generation in the history of humankind. We have books, podcasts, television, movies, newspapers, emails, social media, radio, and satellite radio. Advertisements are everywhere. Our phones listen to our conversations for keywords to sell us more based on our interests. If you have not watched The Netflix documentary, *The Social Dilemma*, written and directed by Jeff Orlowski,[26] I highly recommend it. It will show you all the ways your phone and social media shape your perceptions. Understanding how these pieces of media feed your mindset is critical to the connections you make with other people. Not all media is bad; not all is good. Awareness is what we are after. Part of being an Efficiency Bitch is becoming aware of all the things in your life that shape it and you.

I used to love scary movies and crime investigation shows, until I realized how they were hurting me. With a mother who had a career as a police officer and fraud investigator, I'm aware of the dangers that exist in the world. The constant reminders in my "entertainment," however, started to create unhealthy paranoia. I'm not suggesting you take these shows out of your line-up; you may handle them better than I did. But be mindful in selecting what you watch on television, what you read, and what you view on social media. There is a chance that some of it is creating a subconscious state of panic or paranoia that you don't realize. You are what you consume.

I read once that the words you see, even if you don't read them, soak into your subconscious. Luckily for me, I've always liked motivational signs, t-shirts, and coffee mugs. One day, I decided to organize the apps on my iPhone into little folders, and I had the crazy idea of labeling them according to who I wanted to be, rather than what they were. I changed my folders to read:

- Money → I am generous
- Social Media → I am connected
- Automation → I am productive
- Kids → I am blessed
- News → I am learning
- Health → I am healthy

I did this on my phone and didn't tell anyone. A few weeks later, I noticed my daughter had done the same to her phone. Even if the messages are not ending up in my subconscious, they are ending in my daughter's conscious and I'm perfectly happy about that.

IT TAKES A VILLAGE

You've likely heard, "It takes a village." Or maybe you've seen a coffee mug, t-shirt, or bumper sticker that says, "Your vibe attracts your tribe." You can hang the words in your living room or stick them on a pillow, but until you really understand the truth of these types of statements, you will not be as efficient as you'd like.

Both adages are true. By my definition, your village is all the people you interact with regularly. They are the people you see or speak to daily, the people you live with, the people you work with. Your village is everyone you choose to surround yourself with. Your tribe is a smaller version of your village; they are the people you let into your brain. Your tribe will define your mood, thoughts, and political views.

Think about these two concepts and how they differ from one another. Your village is people you see regularly. They may be friends, coworkers, and advisors. Like it or not, they have an impact on you. The village is constantly changing; people move in and out depending on your life circumstances. These may not be people you see daily, but they influence you regularly. It may also be the media you consume. It's who you follow on social media, the television shows you watch, and the podcasts you listen to.

I am intentional and careful about who is in my village. I've learned this lesson the hard way. On more than one occasion, I've experienced firsthand that not everyone deserves entry into the village. You and only you get to decide who lives in your village. Your village will change a lot over the years. People will come and go. It will grow, then shrink, then grow again.

Think about both the people and the media that are a part of your village. Does your village support you in your current growth? I'm not suggesting that they all think the same way you do. In fact, I'm suggesting the opposite. Do they challenge you and make you better and more well-rounded? One of my oldest friends from high school is on the opposite side of the political spectrum from me, but I love spending time with him (and his amazing wife) and listening to his perspectives. He was a police officer for twenty years and has had experiences I will never understand. The beauty (and apparent rarity) of our relationship is that we can have conversations about really complicated and hard things where we both learn and grow, and never in a way that is shaming, blaming, or disrespectful. These are the types of people I want in my village, and I hope you can find some for yours.

*" Childcare can be unconventional (it takes a village);
do not let judgement from others influence you. You are the best person
to ensure your child's well-being. "*

**Ilse Harley, mother of one,
Regional Vice President and General Manager, Four Seasons Hotels**

FIND YOUR TRIBE

Motivational speaker Jim Rohn famously said that you are the average of the five people you spend the most time with.[27] Your tribe consists of these five people. Have you ever come home from work to find a family member or roommate in a foul mood? Ever noticed how fast that mood rubs off on you? The same thing can happen with habits, slang, beliefs, attitude, and productivity. More than once, I've hung out with people who brought my average down. Although I don't consider myself a drunk or a gossip, when I hang out with people who drink too much, I start to drink too much as well. When I hang out with people who gossip, I fall into these ugly behaviors too. You can't always choose the people in your life, but when you can, choose wisely. There are great people everywhere. Keep looking for them, and don't settle! More importantly, don't stay with them if it's not right for you. If they show you a glimpse of who they are and it sends up a red flag, turn and walk away. People will show you their true colors; it's up to you not to be colorblind.

Do you have a clear picture of who is in your village and your tribe? Are the people in your tribe headed in the direction you want to go, or are they keeping you stuck in the mud? Consider what life would be like if you had the right people in your tribe. Make a quick mental note of areas you want to improve. Now, think about the people you know who have those traits. List the five people you admire and want to become more like. They don't have to be your best friends today. They may be someone you admire. Now, approach them. It doesn't have to be awkward or creepy. It can be a simple email, comment on social media, or text message. Tell them you respect them and want to learn from them. Ask them to be your mentor. I have several mentors. I also mentor several people. Find someone who wants to listen to you and is willing to share candidly about their successes and failures.

If these are already people you are close to, add more time deliberately picking their brains about how they became who they are. Ask questions. Learn from them. Connect. The cool part about using this little math equation (the average of the five people you are with) is that you can decide the amount of time you spend with them and mix it up any way you want. Spend more time with people who have what you want and can show you how to get it. Ask them what they did well and what didn't go well. Learn from their mistakes and replicate their wins.

> *"There has always been someone in my corner. My husband, fellow moms, single friends, patients, employers, and coworkers have all helped me get it done. Choose your people carefully."*
>
> **Hailey Alfred, mother of two**
> **Doctor of Physical Therapy (DPT), Next Level Physical Therapy**

But what if you can't think of a single person you want in your average? Go find them. A great way to do this is to get involved in local groups or clubs for business, moms' groups, fitness, photography, or other hobbies and interests that attract the type of people you want to be with. It's true what they say that birds of a feather flock together. Finding people interested in what you are interested in will inspire you. You will discover very experienced people, inexperienced people, and everyone in between. This will lead to new momentum, new friendships, and spending time with new people. Being near them will likely bring you more people who have a similar growth mindset. Think big. Look for local groups by asking people you admire where they spend time. It can be focused on career, education, kids, sports…anything.

When I first became a mom, I didn't know what I didn't know. To learn, I attended free breastfeeding support groups at the hospital. I learned quickly which moms were like me and which were not. I asked the moms I wanted to be like what Mommy and Me classes they attended, and I went too. I repeated that cycle through the toddler years and the addition of new children. (P.S., your baby doesn't know if you're doing it right or wrong either. Make sure they feel loved, you feel happy, and the rest will sort itself out.)

The same holds true as I started on my path of building a business, launching a podcast, and writing this book. I wanted to learn from the people who were doing what I wanted to be doing, so I brought them into my tribe. And let me be clear. I didn't walk up to a stranger or person I hardly knew and say, "Hey, I'm adding you to my tribe so I can be your average." That would be weird. Instead, I paid attention to them, asking them questions, taking their advice, watching them, and absorbing their greatness. People sense if you are being disingenuous. This is not a selfish, greedy, or fake approach to making friends. It's a recommendation on how to find people to learn from. They'll learn from you too!

One of the more difficult things about being a young woman who wants to have a family and a badass career is that too few women have done it before us. It is difficult to be what you can't see and to find people to connect with for this average to work. Fortunately, the world is much more accessible than it used to be, thanks to the Internet. If you can't find five people through traditional routes, look for alternative methods. LinkedIn is a great jumping-off point to look for inspiration.

The people you live with may or may not be part of the average of five you want in your tribe, but they are in your village. They have an impact on you. If the people in your home are not supportive of your dreams, it's ok. They may not see what you see. While it's true that you cannot make people change, you can start to change your behaviors. Your positive new behaviors will rub off on them. As you increase your "number," their average will also increase because of their own average of five equation. And if not, that's ok too. Having someone in your home who wants to keep you from growing or changing is a challenging obstacle to overcome, but it's not impossible. It can be difficult not to put your expectations on other people. Cry, beg, fight as you might, they are in control of their own behaviors. Keep your expectations of yourself high, hold yourself accountable, and don't give up. You can only change how you manage a situation, your reaction to it, and your resolution. Loving someone does not mean you have to agree with them. And disagreeing with them does not mean you don't love them. Dare to think differently, be open to new ideas, and think about ways to improve your life and your children's lives.

"This is the way it's always been" is the most dangerous saying in more than one context. Just because it has been that way doesn't mean it has to continue, but it also doesn't mean the person who stands by the old way is a bad person. Understand that what life taught your mother, aunt, or grandmother is different from what life may be teaching you. The lives of women in past generations were different than yours is today. They are not offering bad advice; it just may be a little outdated. They didn't have as many options, rights, or opportunities as women have today. They may not see things the way you see them, and that's ok. New generations are paving new roads for the future. Keep your eyes on your tribe, increase your average, and let your village come and go as needed. If you need tips on forming a tribe of people, check out *A Tribe Called Bliss* by Lori Harder.[28] She provides a beautiful way to create the tribe of your dreams.

SUPPORT THE CAUSE

I am a product of generations of privileged people, but they were also incredibly generous philanthropists. Giving back, paying it forward, and taking social responsibility are all important to me. I want to share my knowledge, my time, and my money, when possible, with those less fortunate or organizations that are bettering the world. Countless ways exist to get involved in your community, many of which double as an opportunity to increase your "average," efficiency and happiness. Start by looking for activities that interest you. If you are an expert in a particular field, offer your knowledge. If you want to learn about a specific topic, attend an online lecture. If you want to support a cause, consider donating money or supplies. The trick is finding the right place to volunteer and determining how much time to offer.

As a young mom, I thought I needed to volunteer for everything. I had this imaginary audience following me around, judging every little decision I made. The audience never had a single face, but rather the faces of every-one I'd ever known or seen. I became the actor on stage performing for this imaginary audience. Every whim they called out became a new way I had to prove my worth as a mom: "breastfeed for a year," "make your own baby food," "use cloth diapers," "keep your house immaculate," "cook dinner ev-ery night," "be an incredible wife," "don't get fat," "make a lot of money," "get a Master's degree," and "do it all with one hand tied behind your back while standing on your head." Whenever someone in the imaginary audience yelled out, I took it as a command.

The first year my daughter attended kindergarten, her teacher asked me if I would be the room mom. I felt so guilty. This sweet kindergarten teacher who taught not only mine but a room full of five-year-olds asked *me* to help *her*. How could I possibly turn her down? Did I have time? No! I had a full-time job and three kids under five, but I said yes anyway. Guess what I didn't know? She wasn't asking me because she wanted *me*. She asked everyone.

Then we received a letter about Girl Scout registration. My daughter wanted to join, so we attended the meeting. Want your kid to join a troop? Great! But you have to be the leader. Hook, line, and sinker. By second grade, I was also volunteering as the Parent Teacher Organization (PTO) president. That year I also flew 200,000 airline miles for work. My body felt miserable, but I told myself I needed to contribute. If I don't do it, who will? I let the guilt take over, and it absolutely drained me.

I learned my lesson. Never say "yes" the first time they ask. The request will be sent to everyone. If you don't answer first, chances are good that some-one else will. If no one steps up, they will ask again. Still keep quiet. If you have an interest in the role, think about it. Consider what it will cost you. Sleep? Time with your kids? Your morning routine? Consider the things you will have to move around, drop, or push back to fit this new commitment into your schedule. If you still want to do it, without feeling obligated, call them on your time and your terms and offer to take the role.

This goes for everything. Keep your hand down when your kids play sports, and the coach says, "Who will volunteer to bring snacks tomorrow?" Let the other parents offer first. You can sign up to bring snacks at the end of the season. This way you have time to make space for it. I encourage you to volunteer time, money, and energy, but I believe strongly that it should be on your terms.

Today, I volunteer for lots of things, but I'm intentional about what and how I serve. I'm on the Board of Directors at Planned Parenthood Arizona, an advisory board member at a youth ranch camp, a mentor, public speaker, and guest lecturer. These activities fill my heart and move me towards the goals I have set for myself. I seek out the opportunities I want to participate in, not the other way around. I don't answer the cold call volunteer requests the world seems to throw at me in fistfuls. Instead, I'm deliberate and organized with who and what I volunteer for.

Find organizations or people that serve a purpose you believe in. Consider the types of community involvement you have today. Are any of them no longer a good fit for who you want to become? Consider giving them thirty days' notice to find a replacement for your position. Then, build a list of ways you want to volunteer will excite you, help you meet your goals, and make you a better version of yourself.

Finding ways to give back and share your kindness can be easier than it seems. Many years ago, a Facebook friend posted about her brother's illness and asked her friends to register at Be the Match Bone Marrow Registry. I created an account, had a cheek swab kit sent to my house, and submitted my sample to Be the Match. Ten years went by and nothing happened. In 2022 Be the Match called to inform me of a potential match for a patient with a terminal illness. His best chance of recovery would be a stem cell transplant. The process is complicated, and I fear I might oversimplify it, so I'll just give you the basics. Over the course of one month, I had to get a complete physical, begin injections of a drug called Filgrastim, and then fly to another city for the seven-hour harvest of my stem-cells to donate. The entire process turned out amazing and one I would do again in a heartbeat. Giving someone hope and a second chance at life is such a great experience. I also enjoyed seeing the not-for-profit at work. I had never been part of an organization like Be the Match. I have raised money for these types of organizations at work or donated over the years, but to see magic in action felt awe-inspiring. This is definitely a place I am happy to spend my time, energy, and stem cells.

THE ART OF PERSUASION

One of the best tips I can offer you as an aspiring EB is the art of talking to people so they can hear you. When you are scheduling a doctor's appointment, working on a contract negotiation, or managing conflict, the way you talk to people matters.

To get what you want, you need to be able to articulate what you want. More importantly, you need to communicate in a way that allows the other person to hear you. Communication is a two-way process. You send the message out, and they receive it. If along the path of receiving the news, however, it gets twisted, faded, or distorted, the process and delivery will be incomplete. This is true of everything—from asking for a raise, requesting a refund for a product you bought, or managing other significant decisions like what color to paint the bedroom wall. There are five key factors to ensuring a message is received correctly:

1. **Time and place:** This is the one that I see most people miss time and time again. Even if the message is perfectly articulated, the time and place impact the receiver's ability to understand it. A good rule of thumb is to praise in public and punish in private. This holds true whether you're talking to a friend, partner, kids, or coworkers. No one likes to be publicly humiliated; it's the quickest way for someone to shut down. If it's a sensitive work issue, having one witness is a good idea, but don't make a public spectacle of a private problem. And please, oh please, don't punish by email. If you have feedback to give someone, they deserve to hear it from your tone, voice, body language, and eyes. Give people difficult feedback face-to-face. It's ok to start the conversation with, "I'm nervous / uncomfortable talking to you about this." It will give you both a chance to brace for what comes next and be able to absorb the message.

2. **Be kind:** I often see people talk to each other as if they are reprimanding a dog who chewed their favorite shoes. There is no need to swell up like a gorilla. Stay calm, and the listener will receive your message. I always come in with a smile and an opportunity to laugh. Using a tone that conveys the conversation is a "win/win" situation will land you more wins than if you make it a "win/lose."

3. **Sticks and stones:** Don't use name-calling, swearing, or a raised voice. Leave accusations at the door. Depending on how you grew up, this may take time and constraint, so buckle up. We tend to take on the language patterns and vernacular of those we surround ourselves with (hello, village), so be aware of the words you use. During an argument, my husband once told me that just because I got louder didn't mean I won. He was right. He was unable to hear me when I raised my voice. Saying things in a way that won't make other people put their guard up will help you come closer to an understanding and agreement. Ruth Bader Ginsburg once said, "Fight for what you believe in, but do it in a way that makes others want to follow you." This is the way forward. War has a time and a place. Some ideals deserve to be fought for with every ounce of passion, focus, and determination you can muster. But if the volume is always at ten, people acclimate to the noise and tune it out. These tactics are very effective with people who work in customer service. Consider the beating that employees take in roles like airport security and gate agents or front desk staff at doctors' offices and schools. They become used to dealing with very grumpy people and often put up a tough exterior to get through the day. My goal is to be their favorite transaction of the day.

4. **Say what you mean:** Avoid being passive-aggressive at all costs. Telling someone it's okay when it's not, then coming back later angry about it, will do nothing but send mixed signals. The next time you say something, they will second guess what you

mean. Think about your options and, if needed, ask for more time. Nothing will kill future negotiations faster than a pattern of saying one thing and doing another. Simon Sinek explains that effective confrontation begins with three key elements: Feelings, Behavior, and Impact (FBI).[29] Identify the specific feeling you have, the behavior that caused it, and the impact it will have if it continues. The more specific you can be, the easier it will be for the person to understand. Sinek gives examples of this in an incredible video on YouTube. Search "Simon Sinek Effective Confrontations," and give it a watch.

5. **Use tact:** The definition of tact is "the ability to say or do the right thing without making anyone unhappy or angry."[30] Approach every uncomfortable situation with this important trait and watch your relationships, connections, and persuasiveness change. Being able to tell someone they smell bad or dress inappropriately at work is one of the most uncomfortable things I have ever had to say to another human being. As a manager, I've had to do this at least a dozen times. I'm sure I scared the other person the first time I did it. I was scared too. I fumbled my words and felt awkward. The last time I did it, the person returned to me later and thanked me for delivering such a difficult message so gently. This was when I realized that how I talked to people impacted my ability to lead and affect change. Brené Brown, a noteable shame researcher, has written several valuable books. My favorite, which discusses giving feedback, is *Dare to Lead*. She has a resource on her website called "Dare to Lead, The Engaged Feedback Checklist."[31] Number ten on her checklist reads, "I can model the vulnerability and openness I expect to see from you." It's that simple. Find the right mindset to approach any conflict or negotiation by offering others the vulnerability you would like to see from them.

At some point, you'll need to use the art of persuasion to convince someone to see your side of an argument and agree to change their mind. In these cases, understand the other person's perspective better than your own. Consider their pain points. Argue with yourself about why they are right, and you are wrong. This is one of the best trainings that lawyers receive. They are trained to see cases objectively and learn how to defend or prosecute both sides of the same topic. I do this in many areas of my life, including political issues and social injustice issues. I won't solidify my stance on an issue until I fully understand the argument of both sides. Understanding someone else's perspective is the best way to win them over and maybe even shift their opinion.

Use this same approach at work when asking for a promotion or raise. According to Indeed's Hiring Lab,[32] only 58 percent of women report being comfortable asking for a promotion. In contrast, more than 74 percent of men are comfortable asking for a promotion. This gap exists because men have generations of experience, whereas women do not. Now it's our turn. Brainstorm why you deserve a promotion or raise. Think of all the reasons why your employer will agree *and* may not agree. Inventory the items that make you valuable at your job. During the conversation, bring up the possible objections and solutions before they have a chance to.

Intimate relationships often create a new type of connection. Knowing how to communicate love in a way your partner can receive is important for a happy life together. *The 5 Love Languages: The Secret to Love that Lasts*, by Gary Chapman, explains this concept in detail.[33] The five main ways that humans give and receive love are physical touch, acts of service, words of affirmation, gifts, and quality time. The crazy part, and what's so valuable about this information, is that we give love the same way we receive it. If you feel most loved when someone gives you a thoughtful gift, while your partner feels most loved through words of affirmation, the expensive gift you buy them won't mean as much as if you tell them how important they are to you. Knowing your partner's love language and speaking to them in it helps to build a lasting connection.

These types of communication don't only count in romantic relationships. Telling a person how much you care about them is critical to any relationship and connection. Simple things like remembering a friend's birthday, asking to see pictures of their vacation, and attending their child's first birthday party are part of a bonding experience. If, by contrast, you never respond to their text messages, can't be bothered to attend their baby shower, and only call when you need something, you're inevitably sending a different message to them. Relationships and connections will not stand the test of time without effort, energy, and intention.

The way you treat people matters. The way you show them you care matters. The longer you have relationships, the more critical they are to nurture. Social media has made it very easy to stay connected to people without seeing them all the time, but only if you engage. Watching their social media feed as a bystander may make you feel connected to them, but I promise you they don't know you are smiling when you see the picture of their children. They don't even know you saw it.

Maintaining a connection with others will not only give you new opportunities to learn and grow but will also keep your spirit alive and happy. The old saying, "People buy from people," means humans typically engage with, purchase, or follow a person rather than a product. If you want more information on ways to negotiate, read *Never Split the Difference: Negotiating as If Your Life Depends on It*, by Chris Voss. It's a game-changer.[34] Voss refers to a concept called the "I am Normal" paradox. It's the assumption that others see things the same way you do and that you are the normal one. If we all experience life differently, however, there is no normal and we cannot see through the same lens. Hence, none of us is normal.

My mission in life is to always be willing to learn new ideas from others' opinions and experiences. I have taken on this multi-perspective approach in everything I do. Maybe it's the accountant in me, but I look at both sides of the equation before I solve for true. Politics, religion, money management, raising children—all of it is 100 percent opinion-based. Even writing that statement is my opinion. Today's world is so overwhelmed by easy access to information that sometimes no one can tell what is fact and what is opinion. Access to this information can be helpful if you are looking to learn someone's perspective, but hurtful if you take their opinions as facts. One thing is for sure: social media proves there is no such thing as normal.

Take what you have learned in this chapter and apply it to all your relationships. One of the incredible opportunities that we have, as humans, is the ability to build relationships and support one another—and it all starts with connection.

"My mother told me to 'choose your friends wisely because you can't choose your family'."

Jacque Humphreys, mother of three
Financial Fraud Investigator

CHAPTER 6

H for HARMONY

Now that you know how to be efficient in money, time, inboxes, and human connection, let's talk about how to make them all work together. Without one key element, you will never stop swimming upstream: Harmony. For me, harmony means all things working in sync, ebbing and flowing as needed. It means shifting gears smoothly and knowing that nothing needs to be perfect so long as you keep moving.

The buzzword of the last decade or so has been "balance." We are bombarded with permission slips from self-care coaches who promise to teach us the magic of balance and fast fixes. Balance, while both well-meaning and a sales pitch, implies that you need to do something equally on both sides. The corporate world has doubled down on this through initiatives that remind us of the need for work/life balance. I've never related to that. It implies I need to compartmentalize my job, family, self, home, and hobbies. It makes me picture dividing myself and my day into five parts and somehow balancing them within those limits. Additionally, it means that work is half my day, and all the other components together are supposed to add up to the other half. Why do I want my job to be fifty percent of my life? For a long time, I thought this is what I was supposed to do. I gave it all I had. I filled my calendar and to-do lists on the "life" side so it would equal the work I had to do on the "job" side. Then, one day, it snuck up on me. It turned into a badge of honor.

I could recite my "have to" list in a way that would make you feel sorry for me. You would hear my story and know I worked hard because I did it all and stood strong. Damn it, I was balanced! But I was also miserable. I wasn't doing it intentionally or consciously. Society's expectations of a working mom were reason enough. The invisible workload weighed heavily on my shoulders. Everything around me told me that I had to be Supermom. One day, Supermom tried to kill me.

The new buzzword surrounding working women is "burnout." I began to recognize the stress-response loop that I could not break, and that I might be addicted to it. Stress in life is not a bad thing; in fact, I think it's a good thing when done in the right way. The problem is I didn't know how to identify and manage stress. Instead, I piled it on. To cope, I would find ways to numb myself. Some people do this through food, television, drugs, or alcohol. I numb myself by keeping busy. Eventually, the physical impact took hold. A wide variety of symptoms can manifest from prolonged high stress. These symptoms vary to some degree in each of us. I developed headaches, an upset stomach, and the habit of clenching my teeth. These gave way to mood swings, a lowered immune system, and complexion issues. I was perpetually sick with non-stop colds and sinus infections.

Doing everything seemed easy; listening to my body did not. It caused me continual physical damage. When I didn't listen, my body would take me down. For two straight years, I had daily headaches; of those, three to five would be migraines. I saw a neurologist, an ear/nose/throat specialist, and an acupuncturist. I had my hormones and vision checked. I saw a temporomandibular joint (TMJ) specialist and a naturopath. Nothing helped. Finally, a hypnotherapist helped me realize that my stress stemmed from fear of judgment. Once I confronted my fear of judgment and rejection, I could take the next step. And a nap. She's also the one who gave me the courage to start my writing process for building this book.

Recognizing my barriers and the cycle I found myself in was the game-changer I needed. Slowly but surely, I took inventory and made changes. If I wanted to create a life I love, I needed to be intentional and deliberate in creating harmony in my life.

LOCUS OF CONTROL

"Locus of control" is a concept that explains how a person perceives the events in their life. They perceive that *they* have controlled the events that shaped their life (internal locus), or *something* or *someone* else controlled those events (external locus). If you don't go to the gym today, you might say, "I couldn't go! My alarm didn't go off in time." This is a perceived external locus of control. It was your alarm's fault, something that happened to *you*. Or you might say, "I set my alarm for p.m. rather than a.m., so I missed the gym." This is an internal locus of control.

You will come across people who take no responsibility for the role they play in their own life and others who blame themselves for everything. The purpose here is not to judge, but to take inventory of the way *you* see things. Consider the overall path you see in your life. Do things happen *to* you that you can't control? Or do you have control over things that happen in your life? For me, the answer is both. I can't control some things, but I can control how I respond to them.

After a painful period of growth in my life, I decided that I needed to choose one thing and make a change. One single thing that would impact everything else in my life one way or another. I had to find the lead domino to knock down the next and would ultimately impact change.

Alcohol was that lead domino for me. I have never been the textbook definition of an alcoholic (whatever that is), but I learned its powerful numbing effect. Alcohol made the stress of "the busy" bearable. It also helped me dance, laugh, stay up late, eat, spend money, stay in bed until noon, and miss time with my kids. While I thought it made me relax, it instead chipped away at my life, sanity, and health.

I've been alcohol-free for three years as of the time of this publication, and I still hesitate to talk too much about my decision to no longer drink alcohol. I've felt the other side of that coin. When I drank, I used to think people who didn't drink were preaching, that they were judging me for drinking, and that they placed themselves on a pedestal. I want you to know I know this. I understand how uncomfortable it can be for me to tell you that one of the most critical and best things I did to change my life was to quit drinking. I'm not saying leaving alcohol behind could be that lead domino for you, but it might be.

No matter what your lead domino is, you will find your reference point and start a new path. By making this one change, you place your locus of control into your own hands.

If you have ever considered removing alcohol from your life and need a place to start, I highly suggest two resources. First, check out Sober Sis, founded by Jennifer Kautsch.[35] I've had Jenn on my podcast a few times, and I love the way she helps women become sober-minded. She has fantastic tools to help reset and learn what life is like without "wine o'clock." Secondly, I highly recommend Annie Grace's book, *This Naked Mind: Control Alcohol, Find Freedom, Discover Happiness & Change Your Life.*[36]

Jenn and Annie are both gentle and educational in their approach. Neither uses shame or fear. They teach the science of what our brains and bodies experience when we consume alcohol. Even one drink has a significant impact on hormones that perpetuate anxiety and stress. I went into my sober life with the intent of trying to make it through a dry January. When February arrived, I realized how good I felt and decided to try one more month. Years later, I have no intention of going back. I've found things I love to supplement the social feelings associated with alcohol. I drink non-alcoholic beer and hop water. I love sparkling water with a splash of Fire Brew. This tricks your brain into releasing the feel-good hormones you crave. I'll leave this section with encouragement to try one month without alcohol. I hope you see the massive change I did.

TRY NEW THINGS

In my junior year of college, I saw a poster for a Walk Disney World internship. I went to an information session and got an interview. Four months later, I was on my way to Orlando, the first time I left the state of Arizona without my family, feeling confident and excited. I don't remember the flight, but I do remember how I felt two hours after landing—terrified. I called my mom, sobbing. This is the only thing I remember her saying: "Try it for two days. If you hate it, I'll fly you home on Wednesday." That was all I needed to hear. Nothing would be set in stone; it could be undone if I needed it to be. Since that internship, I've used that thought every time I've done something scary. When I moved alone to Hawaii, when I took a new role at corporate, when I flew alone to China, when I started my business, and even when I started writing this book.

Take the chance. See what happens. You can always undo it or say stop later. It's the same advice I give to young women who I mentor: "Take that crazy international job assignment now while you're single and have no kids. You'll have to come back, because of work visas, and if you wait, you may never take the risk." When making decisions, don't paint yourself into a corner. Give yourself choices and options. The only things certain in life are death and taxes. Everything else is up for grabs.

> **"** *Find the beauty in imperfection! Not only is perfection impossible,*
> *it's also an opportunity for teaching as a parent. It's important for*
> *kids to see their parents work to solve problems, make mistakes*
> *(and move forward from them), and be beginners at new things.* **"**
> **Anna Finn, mother of two**
> **Lawyer**

MOM WARS

Before I had kids, I still sensed the elephant in the room regarding working moms. As a child, I felt the difference between the stay-at-home moms who picked up their kids right after school and the working moms who picked up their kids from after-school care between five and six o'clock. Once I entered the workforce, I felt it again. The moms and non-moms didn't sit together at lunch. Those without kids felt the moms took shortcuts or dipped out early, always using a pick-up time as an excuse. Non-moms would stay late and complain in silence that the moms did not work as hard as the rest.

Then, I became a mom and saw both sides clearly. Working moms, at least ones like me, are stuck between two worlds: working like she doesn't have children and trying to be a mom like she doesn't have a job. I would drop the kids off at daycare and haul ass to work. I would slide into my office at 8:01 a.m., work as quickly as possible, eat the fastest lunch, and run out the door at 5:00 p.m., bringing work home with me to do after the kids went to bed. No one could see the pressure I felt. No one ever does because they're too busy managing their own life. It's like going to a group fitness class. Some people are so afraid of it and so worried they'll look dumb trying yoga for the first time, but most people don't notice anyone else. When I'm in a group fitness class, I'm so focused on myself, Oprah Winfrey could be doing yoga next to me, and I wouldn't notice.

The challenges differ depending on where you work, whether you have a spouse, and whether you have kids. Life as a single parent or a child with neurodiversity can add other types of stressors for both parents and children. The type of home you have impacts the stress your carry. Maybe you live in a mobile home, apartment, city high-rise, farmhouse in the country, planned community, or military base. The bottom line is we all work hard and have challenges. Comparing ourselves to one another will only make things more difficult.

It doesn't matter if you are a working mom or stay-at-home mom; mom life is hard. It doesn't matter if you have kids or not, building a career is hard. So why do we make it harder by fighting each other? Mom wars are real. I see it all the time. Sometimes it's obvious, and sometimes it's passive, like memes on social media. Everyone wants to defend their choices by making others feel bad for them.

The war between moms and non-moms at work isn't where it ends. There are battles between working moms and stay-at-home moms too. I have felt this pressure on school spirit days, when planning birthday parties, and even when planning a home-cooked meal. Comparison and competition are not helpful. What if we all came together to focus on what we each do well, and not shame one another for her choices?

Women of past generations had access to only a few people, usually their moms, sisters, and a few friends or neighbors. Today, thanks to social media, we have access to many women, complete strangers, all over the world. These women have different experiences, different versions of their truth, and different family backgrounds. Social media has been an incredible learning tool as I grew and learned new tricks as a parent. I could lean into social media when I needed advice and give back as I found new tips and tricks that helped me. I discovered my passion for helping other women navigate the same paths I had been down in a social media group dedicated to moms with infants that my sister and I created.

I have never met a parent who says they have it all figured out, they never get frustrated, or they don't have days when they want to run and hide. Everyone has different levels of involvement with their children. Every family looks different. Every family has various resources, but I promise you that everyone knows parenting is hard. Period. Some phases are more complex than others. Today, I feel like I'm in the easiest stage of parenting. My kids are at fun ages: seven, nine, and eleven. They are all potty trained, sleep through the night, can read and make their own snacks, and generally keep themselves out of harm's way. They are busy, interested in things, have homework, and are learning how the world works.

At one point, I had three kids in five-point harness car seats. Getting them in the car took at least ten minutes. They were more demanding of me physically. They needed help bathing, using the bathroom, and getting dressed. But they had fewer extracurricular activities, no homework, and no friends saying mean words that left wounds.

I see what's coming next. I'm staring down the barrel of three kids in their teenage years. Hormones, attitude, puberty, and broken hearts are right around the corner. My brain can't fully understand what these days will look like, or maybe I just can't let myself imagine them. Still, I look forward to the support other women will give me as I enter these years.

One fascinating and sad outcome of the COVID-19 pandemic has been dubbed the "she-session." Women left the workforce in droves due to unavailable and unreliable childcare. Since pay is still not equal, it often made more sense for the dad to keep working and the mom to leave the workforce. It will take decades for women to make up as much of the workforce as we did before COVID-19. One amazing outcome of the COVID-19 crisis is new acceptance of working from home and the creation of "side hustles."

Almost everyone I know has some version of a side hustle. It's never been easier and more tolerated by large corporations. I found my voice in my podcast, which developed my side hustle during COVID-19, and it's one of the best things I've ever done. It brought me to you through writing this book. I didn't have more time in the day. In fact, I had less since the kids were at home learning virtually. But I found passion, excitement, and self-worth that I had never felt before. Being a working woman can mean anything you want it to mean, and you can do it from anywhere like no other time in history. I, for one, am thrilled.

When I travelled frequently for work, I was asked two questions all the time, almost exclusively from women: "Who's watching your kids?" and "Do you feel safe?"

Who is watching my kids?! Burn. Please don't ask a road warrior woman this question. It's riddled with judgement and guilt. Their *father* is watching our kids! Yes, he has a full-time job, and yes, he's fully capable. You can probably tell from my tone that this one still stings. I feel the other woman's judgement, hear her inner monologue and criticism saying, "I could never leave my kids alone. Why do you do that?" My answer is simple:

1. **Their father is capable.** If he's not, help get him there. If he's uncomfortable, it's only because it's new to him. Talk to him about it and start giving him the opportunity to learn. Teach him and let him fly. At the beginning of my work travel career (when my kids were two-and-a-half and nine months of age), my mother-in-law would come help occasionally too. By the time our kids were two, four, and six, my husband had the kids on lockdown.

2. **Your kids need to be without you.** Your kids need to experience life without Mom hovering over their every move. As my mom says, "You are raising them to be adults, not raising them to be kids." I believe it's not what you do for your children but what you teach them to do for themselves that will make them awesome adults.

3. **The more life experiences you have, the better mom you will be.** You will have more to offer your kids, more to show them, more to tell them. Go see the world. Try new things and follow your light.

As for, "Do you feel safe?" The answer is yes and no. I don't ever feel totally safe. Being a woman is inherently dangerous. I don't feel safer in Denver than I do in New Delhi. I don't feel safer in Santa Barbara than I do in Hong Kong. I'm not paranoid, but I'm aware of my surroundings at all times. I don't walk alone at night. I don't get into an elevator (or stay in an elevator) if there's just one man in it. I pay attention to the mood, tone, and behaviors of the people around me. I get in the car, lock the doors, and never sit idle in my car on my phone. I do my best to keep myself out of situations where I have no way out. For the record, I freaking *hate* that this is reality, but it is. I just had a conversation with my kids about this recently. It was hard to watch their faces as they processed the information. The world will not be safe for women until men allow it to be. We must continue having this conversation with both boys and girls to move the needle.

Not too long ago, I walked alone to meet a friend for lunch in Seattle, Washington, where a man began following me close behind. He started getting very near my left hand where I carried my wrist wallet. I moved; he moved. I crossed the street; he did too. Based on the visual I had on him, he seemed to be in his mid-fifties, homeless, and looking to take my wallet from me in broad daylight. My heart started racing, but I had considered many times before what I would do if I ever encountered a situation like this.

I started to approach a group of people, but something stopped me as I noticed it was a group of only men. Next, I saw a coffeeshop with its door open. I knew if I slowed down to open a door, he would be close enough to grab my bag, so this open door seemed like my only chance. As I went in, he continued down the street. As I turned to make sure he had gone, I saw he held a cheap steak knife behind his back. Definite confirmation that he had planned to mug me. I sat in the coffee shop for a minute to catch my breath and called my friend to come get me.

He would have taken my wallet had I not been paying attention. I'm sure of it. Safety is not about carrying pepper spray, an alarm, or a gun. It's about being aware of what's going on around you and the situations that can develop out of thin air.

As scary as my story was for me, you may have your own story, or you know someone who has experienced much worse. If you have been the victim of a crime or abuse and need help, contact the authorities in your area or at **womenshealth.gov.**

GLASS BALLS

People often use the phrase "juggling act" to describe their lives. What I've come to realize is that most of the balls we juggle are rubber…they bounce if dropped. If you don't clean your home, it may get dusty, and you may not function normally, but nothing terrible will happen immediately. If you drop your rubber balls from time to time, it's no big deal. You can pick them up later and keep on keeping on.

Some balls are glass, though. If you drop a glass ball, it will break. If it doesn't shatter, it'll get cracked or chipped and cut you when you pick it back up. Your physical and mental health are two of your most essential glass balls. You only have one body. You only have one mind. You only have one life. You risk dropping these balls if you don't take them seriously. The more you take on, the higher the likelihood that you will start dropping balls. The imbalance of the juggling act can happen without you even noticing it.

When I hit rock bottom, I realized I had let my health "ball" fall many times. It had several large cracks and chips in it. I took a step back and looked at all the balls I'd been juggling. I realized quickly I was juggling so many balls, and some didn't even belong to me! Why did I decide to take responsibility for all these extra things that belonged to my husband, employer, friends, strangers, and kids? As I examined my life, I took inventory and filtered out what I could.

My health needed improvement first. My physical health suffered because I prioritized bad habits instead of good habits. A friend of mine posted on social media about a new product she used to improve her health. Desperate for a solution, I contacted her. I won't mention the company name because recommending supplements and protein shakes seems like something that could change quickly. You might be reading this book ten years after I wrote it, and the quality of the product has gone way down. If you want to know what I use today, email me. I'd be happy to share.

This new line of products recommended by my friend changed my health for the better. First, I adopted a daily greens supplement. I found one in powder form, which I added to water and drank. I hate most vegetables. This powder proved to be something tangible that I could add to my daily diet without changing anything else: one step in the right direction of making a positive change. Next, I incorporated one protein shake a day. Then I added multi-vitamins. Eventually, intermittent fasting became part of my routine. Step by step, I improved my health, weight, and fitness. I went from being 100 percent sedentary to lifting weights three times a week, running four days a week, and being in the best physical shape of my life. These changes didn't improve my life in ten minutes, but I started to feel the difference within ten days. From swollen and tired to energetic and active, the benefits did not stop there. My mental fog lifted, my menstrual cycles regulated, and my sleep became more effective than ever before.

I encourage you to take one step. Do one thing today that can become an easy habit and help you build momentum. Find a good greens powder, protein shake, or multi-vitamin, and give it ten days. Be aware that not all products are created equal. You get what you pay for, so use good judgment. If you can't afford the product, collect money in your second pocket and move towards it. Get a little closer today than you were yesterday. You are worth it. Here are some tips for increasing your fitness:

- **Track your food**. I like free apps like MyFitnessPal.[37] You can use its extensive food library to track foods and their macronutrients and calories.
- **Have a daily protein goal.** A good plan is to eat half your body weight in grams of protein every day. Protein fills you up and enables you to build healthy muscle. For example, if you weigh 180 lbs., eat 90 grams of protein.
- **Have a daily water goal.** Drink half your body weight in ounces of water every day. For example, if you weigh 180 lbs., drink 90 ounces

of water. I live in Arizona, so my goal is always a gallon of water a day. It sounds like a lot, but it's easier than it sounds. A great way to build this habit is to get a one-gallon water bottle. Fill it up in the morning and drain it by bedtime. You will pee a lot in the first few days, but your body will get used to it. You'll also notice your skin and digestive system will improve, and you'll have more energy. It's amazing how something so simple can help so much. My husband does not care for plain water, so he adds flavor or electrolyte powder to his. Just be sure you find one that isn't full of sugar.

- **Have a daily calorie goal.** If you are trying to watch your weight, a good rule of thumb is to multiply your body weight by ten. If you weigh 180 lbs., you should eat 1,800 calories every day to function. From there, if you want to maintain, lose, or gain weight, you need to make adjustments. Of course, these are very general and should always be discussed with a physician. Also remember that where your calories come from matter. Five hundred calories from chicken breast are not the same as a piece of cake. All in moderation and harmony.

- **Sleep.** For the love of all that is good in the world, sleep! Rest must be a priority. Make it a non-negotiable, essential part of your day. I use a free app on my Apple Watch to track my sleep, measure my heart rate, and help me interpret my sleep patterns. Other tools are out there depending on your budget and goals. Knowing my numbers helps me monitor and make changes as I need to.

The night after I wrote this chapter, my seven-year-old woke me up in the middle of the night three times. I laughed at my ability to deny the truth that I never sleep through the night. One of my kids wakes me up every night. Sleep disruption is real for parents, and I know as my kids move into their teenage years, they will keep me up at night in different ways. Despite this, I encourage you to adjust your sleep schedule or routine to make sure you get the sleep you need. I often go to bed at 9:30 p.m., but there are days when I fall asleep at 8:00 p.m. Most mornings I wake up at 5:00 a.m., but there are days I'm up at 6:30 a.m. or

7:00 a.m. None of it is perfect, but I always remember that my sleep needs to be a top priority.

- **Move your body every day.** I have a desk job, so getting 10,000 steps is not always easy. I start my day by moving as much as possible. One tool that has helped me is WayBetter.[38] In this app, you play games against other people. For example, you search for games being played that start next week. 1,000 people join the fun. The buy-in is thirty dollars. The game has rules, such as six weeks of jogging three days a week at a minimum pace of an eighteen-minute mile. If you don't do it, you lose your thirty dollars. If you do, you split the pot with the people who did. In most games, I win all my money back plus a few dollars. The motivation is not losing the thirty dollars I put in. The added five dollars I win is my reward for not giving up.

At the end of the day, the idea is not about having a rigid schedule that adds more stress to your life. Don't add to the invisible load. Instead, take on the ideas and actions that are right for you and will improve your life tomorrow. Remember that it is possible to make small changes that will allow you to do more of what you love. Try to add one new idea to your daily routine today. Tomorrow or next week, add another. As you start to feel better, you will find it's easier to sustain your new and improved routine. Do something today that will make your future self feel amazing.

"Make sure to prioritize your own self-care.
It's hard to fill everyone else's cup when your own is not full."

Allison Jackson, mother of two
Founder, Allison Jackson Fitness

CONCLUSION
FALL IN LOVE WITH YOUR FUTURE SELF

The end is my favorite part of any project. I love the wrap-up. The satisfaction of knowing that not only did I start something new, but I completed it too. Plus, I get to check it off my list, one of my all-time favorite things to do.

Now that we are at the end, let's clean up our workspace. Use the things you have learned and build upon them every chance you get. Fall in love with your future self and help her have the best life you can imagine and most definitely deserve.

As soon as you put down this book, start a list of all the things you want. Write down everything your children (born or un-born) deserve, can have, and may want, too. Now make it happen! Take one step today that helps your future self obtain those things. Find the efficiency in everything you do. Spend twenty minutes today hanging a key holder near the backdoor so your future self never has to look for keys again. Put regular deliveries on auto-ship. Listen to the Efficiency Bitch Podcast, send me an email, or go back and skim through the chapters to remember suggestions. Wander through **EfficiencyBitch.com/Favorite Things**. Write down one thing from each of the five pillars (B.I.T.C.H.) to get you started. Commit to completing one of these tasks each day this week. Build a habit. Download one of the books I mentioned to listen to on Audible when you're in the car. Take a step, decide to move forward, and start living your best life.

The world is different today than it was when I started writing this book in early 2020. In the last two years the political, social, professional and health landscape of the United States and the world has been forever changed by the COVID-19 pandemic. And I've experience change in my personal life too.

My husband left his job a few months ago to work for Two Sense Consulting and help bring our family closer together—and offer our family a ton of support at home. The point is nothing lasts forever, the world is always changing. To master becoming an Efficiency Bitch you will have to always be ready for the next right thing, the next evolution and the next thing that will make your future self-happy.

Remember how far women have come. The women who came before us would be so proud (and shocked) at how much influence and equality we have achieved. But also remember the mission is far from over. We have a responsibility to push for more for our children and their children. We must bring men with us, make them our allies and let them see why trust and respect are mutually exclusive. We must teach our sons and daughters that the world is a fantastic place full of opportunities for everyone. We must continue to protect our young and maintain our tenacity. We must remember what we stand for and begin the next phase of feminism as a new kind of bitch. An Efficiency Bitch.

Efficiency Bitch™ (n.): A strong woman who is unstoppable in the pursuit of her dreams. An Efficiency Bitch (EB) is a positive influence.

She refuses to let gender norms, pressure from political ideologies, and cultural stigmas define her goals and life path. She uses self-reflection, others' ideas, and her instincts to drive change.

She strives for maximum productivity with minimum wasted effort or expense. She chooses the people in her life carefully and never allows anyone to dim her light. She manages her life to spend time with her family, her passions, and herself. She lifts others up, demanding the same level of expectation and opportunity.

She counts her blessings and knows that her life is different from everyone else's. She understands where she came from and knows where she is going. She takes responsibility for her path, her choices, and her future.

ACKNOWLEDGMENTS

I thought the book writing process was hard—until I started to write the acknowledgements. Making sure that I fully express my love, gratitude, and appreciation for everyone who has helped me on my writing journey may be my most daunting task yet. I am not a writer. I'm an extroverted accountant, a rare breed who thinks in numbers, and usually out loud. I process new ideas, problems, and thoughts by talking to anyone who will listen, not by writing them out. This journey has been anything but easy for me. I would like to thank each of you who have been part of that sounding board through my process.

To Keli, for giving me the courage to start and helping me begin to cure my fear of judgment.

To Chris, for giving me the inspiration to see it come true and talking me through the steps of book writing when I didn't know where to begin. Chris wrote, *Raising LGBTQ Allies, A Parent's Guide to Changing the Messages from the Playground.* An absolute must read.

To my parents, for listening to every single thought that came into my head as I researched, reworked, and considered every angle. You have probably heard this book one hundred times and still offered to be some of the first to read and offer feedback. Not only are you amazing parents, but also the best kind of friends.

To my husband, Steve, thank you for your support in this insane process. It's been a lot of work. You gave me space when I needed it, read chapters when I asked, and even helped me rename the "Connection" chapter. You are my one and only, and I am so glad you are the one I get to do life with.

To my business partner, Liann, for being the first and only person who got to read my "shitty first draft." I don't know how to describe the type of synergy I feel working with you. We have always been a great team. I'm so grateful to call you my business partner and one of my very closest tribe members.

To my mother-in-law, Chris, thank you for always helping me see the other side of things. You have a unique leadership quality that is inspiring and enlightening. I admire and appreciate you so much. Also, thank you for making my amazing husband.

To Jared, thank you for helping me stumble though the building blocks of creating Two Sense Consulting, including the beautiful design of **TwoSenseConsulting.com** and **EfficiencyBitch.com.** You have been an awesome business partner and friend, and I'm forever grateful. If you are reading this and need a great website designer, look up Kodeak Digital Media Experts.

To Taunya, thank you for teaching me about the concept of saving money. Visualizing the four pockets for saving money has helped me a great deal, and I hope it helped those who read this book. You are amazing!

To Janelle, my amazing admin and podcast editor. You have been such an awesome support to me and somehow read my mind perfectly. I don't always articulate what I want or need, but you have done an amazing job helping me in this process. Thank you for always giving me your opinion, leading with style, and being you.

To the EM Moms Facebook group. As a collective group, you've helped me as I was launching my podcast and writing this book. As funny as it may sound to thank a group of Facebook users, I truly value your feedback.

To Renee, thank you for my logo concept for both the Efficiency Bitch Podcast and Two Sense. You helped me turn my idea into a reality for "my bee". You're very talented.

To the women who offered their beautiful advice throughout the book. Your wisdom and willingness to share is one of my favorite things about this book. I appreciate you and admire you all.

To Laura, my publisher. I knew the first time I met you that you were the right publisher for me. I needed someone to give it to me straight and keep me from putting out a product that was less than great. Your attention to detail, tenacity, and honesty are so appreciated and shine in this book. Thank you for all you did to make this book what it has become and for bringing such a strong team of editors, artists, and publishing professionals to the process.

To Jana, my cover artist. Your talent is beyond impressive. You turned my confusing vision into a cover I truly love. Thank you for knowing what I wanted when I couldn't see it myself.

To Alisa and Taryn, my editors. Thank you for taking this amateur, first-time author's words and helping me learn to form sentences into something I am truly proud to publish. Your job is not an easy one, though I imagine amusing at times. Thank you for not laughing at me and for making me feel confident that I had what it took to turn my scribbles into a book.

To Rachel, Darius and Sara. Thank you for making me look so good in my photos. You know how to make a girl look good.

To all the amazing pre-readers, those who offered Advance Praise and became part of my launch team. Thank you! You were critical to the success of this book and helping me spread my message to those who want to hear it.

To all my friends and family who gave me support, showed excitement for my book, and cheered me on—thank you. Writing a book is the scariest thing I have ever done. As I've told many of you, I feel like I'm carefully planning a party (just the way my mom taught me), and my biggest fear is that no one comes (that is, no one reads it). At the same time, I'm also super scared that people will come and won't like the food (thinking I'm crazy). Thank you for helping me push through my imposter syndrome and take one step at a time.

To you, the reader, whether I included you in the list above or not. Thank you for spending your precious time and money on this book. I hope (with every fiber of my being) that you've enjoyed this book and have learned even just one thing that will make your future self incredibly happy.

ABOUT THE AUTHOR

Raised in Tucson, Arizona, Melissa Leon is a wife, mother of three young children, twenty-plus-year finance professional, and self-proclaimed Efficiency Bitch. After attending Northern Arizona University and earning her Bachelor of Science Degree in Hotel / Restaurant Management, she began a seventeen-year career in luxury hospitality. During that time, she lived in Sedona and Scottsdale, Arizona; Kihei, Hawaii; Miami, Florida; Thousand Oaks, California, and finally settled back in Arizona. While working full-time, Melissa completed her master's degree in Business Administration from Aspen University and her Project Management Professional (PMP) Certification.

Melissa had a unique opportunity to spend ten years in operations finance and seven years in corporate finance managing global projects. She's traveled all over the world, including India, China, Japan, Canada, Mexico, France, Germany, England, and Singapore. She's made new friends everywhere who have inspired and taught her what life is all about—people!

During the COVID-19 crisis, Melissa made the bold decision to leave her hospitality career. She and her longtime friend and colleague opened a fractional CFO and bookkeeping business called Two Sense Consulting. From there, Melissa launched the Efficiency Bitch Podcast and began writing her first book. Melissa has been recognized by KNOW as one of the 40 Over 40 Women to KNOW in America in 2022. She sits on two non-profit advisory boards and mentors young women in search of great careers.

Stay in Touch with Melissa and
Kickstart Your Efficiency Bitch Life Here:

EfficiencyBitch.com/BHive

EfficiencyBitch.com/ActionPlan

EfficiencyBitch.com/FavoriteThings

NOTES

1. Robin DiAngelo, *White Fragility: Why It's so Hard for White People to Talk about Racism* London: Allen Lane, 2019).

2. Robin DiAngelo, *White Fragility: Why It's so Hard for White People to Talk about Racism* (London: Allen Lane, 2019), xiv.

3. "Bitch," Merriam-Webster, accessed June 2, 2020, https://www.merriam-webster.com/dictionary/bitch.

4. *History of Swear Words*, season 1, episode 3, "Bitch," directed by Ves D'Elia, aired January 5, 2021, on Netflix, https://www.netflix.com/title/81305757.

5. Geoffrey Hughes, *Encyclopedia of Swearing: The Social History of Oaths, Profanity, Foul Language, and Ethnic Slurs in the English-Speaking World* (New York: M.E. Sharpe, 2006).

6. Geoffrey Hughes, *Encyclopedia of Swearing: The Social History of Oaths, Profanity, Foul Language, and Ethnic Slurs in the English-Speaking World* (New York: M.E. Sharpe, 2006).

7. "Google Books Ngram Viewer," Google Books (Google), accessed September 23, 2022, https://books.google.com/ngrams/graph?content=bitch&year_start=1915&year_end=1930&corpus=15&smoothing=3&share=&direct_url=t1%253B%252C-bitch%253B%252Cc0.

8. Jo Freeman, "The BITCH Manifesto," accessed April 1, 2021, https://www.jofreeman.com/joreen/bitch.htm.

9. "Family and Medical Leave Act," United States Department of Labor, accessed July 19, 2021, https://www.dol.gov/agencies/whd/fmla.

10. "Maternity Leave: US Policy Is Worst on List of the World's Richest Countries," The Guardian, January 27, 2020, https://www.theguardian.com/us-news/2020/jan/27/maternity-leave-us-policy-worst-worlds-richest-countries.

11. "The Fourth Wave of Feminism," Encyclopaedia Britannica, accessed July 15, 2022, https://www.britannica.com/topic/feminism/The-fourth-wave-of-feminism.

12. "Our Feminist Future," Women's March, accessed August 3, 2021, https://www.womens-march.com/.

13. Stefan Lembo Stolba, "What Affects Your Credit Scores?" Experian, accessed October 26, 2021, https://www.experian.com/blogs/ask-experian/credit-education/score-basics/what-affects-your-credit-scores/.

14. "Stress in America Paying with Our Health," accessed September 15, 2022, https://www.apa.org/news/press/releases/stress/2014/stress-report.pdf.

15. Jill Krasny, "A New Study Shows How Children Are Psychologically Damaged When Parents Fight Over Money," Business Insider, accessed September 10, 2022, https://www.businessinsider.com/a-new-study-shows-how-children-are-psychologically-damaged-when-parents-fight-over-money-2012-1.

16. Laurie Palau, *Hot Mess: A Practical Guide to Getting Organized* (New Hope, PA: zolopublishing, 2017).

[17] Bill Carmody, "Billionaires Master the Rule of 168: Life's Great Equalizer," Inc., June 9, 2016, https://www.inc.com/bill-carmody/billionaires-master-the-rule-of-168-life-s-great-equalizer.html.

[18] Cyril Northcote Parkinson, "Parkinson's Law," *The Economist*, November 19, 1955, https://www.economist.com/news/1955/11/19/parkinsons-law.

[19] "Start Today," accessed January 21, 2020, https://starttoday.com/.

[20] Statista Research Department, "Average Number of Own Children per U.S. Family with Own Children 1960-2020," Statista, July 27, 2022, https://www.statista.com/statistics/718084/average-number-of-own-children-per-family/.

[21] "Census Bureau Estimates Show Average One-Way Travel Time to Work Rises to All-Time High," United States Census Bureau, March 18, 2021, https://www.census.gov/newsroom/press-releases/2021/one-way-travel-time-to-work-rises.html.

[22] Charles Duhigg, The Power of Habit (Batu Caves, Slangor: PTS Publishing House, 2020).

[23] Hal Elrod, *Miracle Morning: The 6 Habits That Will Transform Your Life before 8AM* (London: Hodder & Stoughton, 2018).

[24] "Daily Skimm," theSkimm, accessed January 1, 2020, http://www.theskimm.com/.

[25] Rhona Lewis, "Witching Hour Is the Worst—Here's What You Can Do About It," Healthline, December 20, 2019, https://www.healthline.com/health/baby/witching-hour-baby

[26] *The Social Dilemma*, directed by Jeff Orlowski-Yang (2020; Exposure Labs, Netflix), https://www.thesocialdilemma.com/.

[27] "Success Presents Jim Rohn International," accessed July 21, 2022, https://www.jimrohn.com/.

[28] Lori Harder, *A Tribe Called Bliss: Break Through Superficial Friendships, Create Real Connections, Reach Your Highest Potential.* (New York: Gallery Books, 2019).

[29] Simon Sinek, "Effective Confrontation," Simon Sinek, January 24, 2020, https://www.youtube.com/watch?v=2M_kCCcNDts.

[30] "Tact," Cambridge Dictionary, accessed July 21, 2022, https://dictionary.cambridge.org/us/dictionary/english/tact.

[31] Brené Brown, *Dare to Lead: Brave Work, Tough Conversations, Whole Hearts* (New York: Random House Large Print, 2019).

[32] Ann Elizabeth Konkel, "Gender Gap in Requests for Pay, Promotion Widens in Pandemic," Indeed Hiring Lab, accessed June 8, 2022, https://www.hiringlab.org/2021/03/02/gender-gap-widens-in-pandemic/.

[33] Gary Chapman, *The 5 Love Languages: The Secret to Love That Lasts* (Chicago: Northfield Publishing, 2017).

[34] Chris Voss and Tahl Raz, *Never Split the Difference: Negotiating as If Your Life Depends on It* (London: Random House Business, 2017).

[35] "Sober Sis: Sober-Minded Sisterhood," accessed May 6, 2021, https://www.sobersis.com/ss-home/.

[36] Annie Grace, *This Naked Mind: Control Alcohol, Find Freedom, Discover Happiness & Change Your Life* (London: HQ, 2019).

[37] "MyFitnessPal," accessed July 11, 2022, https://www.myfitnesspal.com/.

[38] "WayBetter," accessed January 1, 2020, https://support.waybetter.com/hc/en-us.

Made in the USA
Las Vegas, NV
08 November 2022

59003168R00083